# REVIEWS

"I thoroughly enjoyed *The Talking Badge*. It is well written and easy to understand and it has a rhythm and a flow that every good book has to have. I can say as a cop, after reading the book, I liked it all. I can also say that anyone who reads this book will know that Mike was a great cop and was and is, a good person." *Anthony Arcado Jr., retired Law Enforcement officer with 30 years of service.*

Often members of the public have an appreciation for what police officers do for their community daily, but rarely do they realize what it takes to do it. The subtitle of Mike's book is so apropos – **"Battle Scars of Police Work."** Many chapters of this book provoked my own recall of certain events and the many challenges encountered during my 30-year career with the Sacramento Police Department, which was primarily spent as a detective. I began my career a few years before Mike Garner, and because I took a different career path than he, we were always "passing ships at sea" with our mutually diverse assignments and working hours. However, Mike's hard-charging and dedicated commitment to fighting crime and catching bad-guys, while exclusively working the streets, was well known throughout our agency and it put him in a unique class of hard-working officers.

Through a series of work related and personal stories, Mike's book does a masterful job of painting a clear picture of how his police assignments molded his viewpoints of society and mankind in general; and collectively how the stress of his numerous sad and dangerous experiences profoundly impacted his personal life. His articulate depictions of many of these stories provide a raw exposure to a full range of emotions, thoughts, challenges, divine intervention, and the cumulative costs that many cops would typically experience under similar circumstances. Yet his moral fiber, largely instilled in him by his parents, coupled with his own life experiences, luck, and profound learning moments on the streets with encounters of disadvantaged individuals, ultimately helped him survive his career, while providing a deep and well-balanced outlook on life and police work in general.

I think this book would serve as a good read for any aspiring police officer, any rookie police officer, or a relative of a police officer.

*Rich Overton*
*Homicide Detective (Ret.)*
*Sacramento Police Department*

An entertaining and interesting insight of police work by a veteran of the Sacramento Police Department. Mike Garner recalls actual events and takes the reader through the challenges facing officers on and off the job. This is a fascinating, enjoyable read.

*Judy Pierce, author of **The Surprising Scary Day: An Albert and Friends Adventure***

As I was reading about the author and his dedication to the care for his mother I had tears in the corners of my eyes. I was thinking when I get to those chapters I will be a mess. We have been taught that our officers in blue are our heros, we forget that they are human and need mental care too. I would definitely buy this book and recommend it to others.

*Marlene Meincke, Champion Beta reader*

# The Talking Badge

## Battle Scars of Police Work

# The Talking Badge

## Battle Scars of Police Work

**Mike Garner**

**Umbach Publishing**

a sub-imprint of
**Samati Press**

The Talking Badge contains true stories and stories drawn from true experiences that were fictionalized for narrative purposes by a cop who worked the streets for thirty years. Names have been changed to protect the guilty and the innocent. Some incidents have been adapted to protect privacy, while still conveying the essence of a police officer's life and work.

CAUTION: Adult language and graphic, sometimes very disturbing content.

ISBN-13 — 978-1-949125-38-2 (Print Version)
ISBN-13 — 978-1-949125-37-5 (Digital versions)
ISBN-13 — 978-1-949125-28-3 (Audio version)

Library of Congress Control Number: 2022915812

Edited by Black Cat Editing Service

Author photo on back cover by Sharon S Darrow
Front cover design by Samati Press

Publisher: Umbach Publishing,
A sub-imprint of Samati Press Sacramento, California

Manufactured in Sacramento, California,
United States of America

# Table of Contents

## Acknowledgements

To My Brother Billy,
Thank you for being there when I needed you.

To My Aunt Barbara,
Thank you for the hours of companionship.

To My Cousin Sam,
Thank you for your words of wisdom

To My Publisher Sharon,
Thank you for believing in my work.

A special thanks to the late Ken Umbach for giving me my start in the writing world and for understanding my perspective in life.

## FOREWORD
**Sam Chan, Ph.D.**

When Mike originally asked me if I'd be willing to write the "Forward" (vs. "Foreword") for his new book, I immediately replied it would be an honor, but cautioned that I might end up writing a "Backward" instead.

Mike is my younger cousin who I grew up and stayed connected with for well over 60 years. In fact, his father, my favorite uncle, was present at my birth. But just twenty-six years later, I recall breaking down at his funeral service and bawled like a baby as I mourned the loss (far too early in life) of my "Uncle Bill" and his brilliant mind, free spirit, and exceptionally wise, compassionate soul.

That soul evolved and lived on in his son Mike. As he describes in Chapter 1 ("My Lost Childhood"), the tragic and traumatic death of his dad at a young age marked the beginning of Mike's journey toward a thirty-year career in law enforcement, protecting and serving as a caregiver for hundreds of people in need and ultimately becoming a selfless caretaker for his mom.

Mike inherited many genes from our beloved Grandpa Garner, a philosopher, toolmaker, craftsman, inventor, and master storyteller. The collection of true (not invented) short stories that Mike tells in the chapters that follow represent three decades of working as a cop on the streets of Sacramento, my hometown.

There may have been "eight million stories in the Naked City" but Mike shares more than eighty stories in the River City. He highlights the profound depth and breadth of these stories in his Introduction.

As noted in the book's subtitle, *"Battle Scars of Police Work,"* Mike reveals many of the emotional scars he acquired with exceptional candor and vulnerability. After twenty years in the Department, following the death by suicide of his partner and old friend, Mike moved on from being a street cop to becoming an instructor.

He began teaching Stress Management in Law Enforcement (SMILE) classes and immediately embraced his skills and passion as a gifted trainer. Apart from the state-of-the-art programs and curricula he developed and presented to dozens of police departments, he acquired an "in-depth knowledge of personal psychology through thousands of hours of self-examination."

From one cop to another, as a peer professional, he was committed to paying it forward (especially reaching out to young

officers) and drove home the message:
*"Knowing how to protect your mind is just as important as wearing your bullet-proof vest."*
This was the space that Mike and I shared our professional contacts, resources, and information. In true form, he closes the book with his grand finale: "The Essence of Life."
Throughout the years, we've exchanged reflections on many subjects: the universe, awe, nature, human and animal behavior, enlightenment, philosophy, religion, politics, systemic racism, and social justice.

While moving freely from the "talking badge" to talking from the couch, Mike has often claimed: "You understand my mind and soul." But, in fact, it's the **mutual** epiphanies, spiritual gifts, and deeply felt personal connections that we've enjoyed as cousins.

I know that his writings and teachings in this book will open every reader's mind, excite them, and touch their hearts with both sorrow and joy. Whether we're in the fields of law enforcement, mental health, any of the helping professions, or throughout the lives we all live, in the words of Father Greg Boyle: *"Our job is to help souls feel their worth."*

**Sam Chan, Ph.D.**
Is a clinical psychologist and former countywide District Chief with the Los Angeles County Department of Mental Health. He

previously held senior administrative and faculty positions at the California School of Professional Psychology, Children's Hospital Los Angeles, the USC School of Medicine, and the UCLA Department of Psychiatry. Dr. Chan focused much of his career on mental health promotion, prevention, and early intervention with culturally and linguistically diverse children and families. He has made significant contributions to transdisciplinary workforce development in the health care, education, and human services fields.

## About The Author

I grew up in Marysville, California. It was a small town much like any other throughout the country. My dad was a lab technician, and my mom was a housewife.

She stayed home and tried her best to raise my older brother, Billy, and myself. We were both out-of-control hell raisers when our dad was at work. We often got into arguments which turned into physical fights, which I lost all the time.

My brother unknowingly made me a tough kid with all his bullying and beat downs. When we were growing up, my brother was mean to me on more than one occasion, but he was also my best friend.

Billy and I would invent games to play in our living room during winter days to keep ourselves occupied. We both loved sports and our house was located directly across the street from a junior high school. We had the biggest front yard any kid could want.

The school yard was extremely large with four separate baseball diamonds with wire backstops and benches. Many tackle football games were played each year in that schoolyard.

Sandlot baseball, football and basketball were big parts of my life. Playing two sports in high school kept me out of trouble. Going to either football or baseball practice every day after school for four years prevented me from hanging around my non-athletic friends, who liked to smoke pot and drink beer.

I hung around a rough crowd growing up. A lot of my friends died violent deaths. Some were shot, stabbed, or died in late night car crashes after one of the large keg beer parties we had each weekend.

Drinking beer and smoking pot became part of my life at an early age. This continued on for many years until I became a cop. The pot smoking had to stop, but unfortunately, the drinking didn't.

I had some close calls growing up and could have been arrested or killed, like several of my close friends. I wasn't a criminal, but I did more than my share of illegal drugs and had fist fights from time to time.

Early one morning, my dad had a heart attack and made one demand before he died in my arms. He looked up at me and said, "Take care of your mom". For the rest of my life, I tried my best to honor his last request.

I soon needed a job because I wanted to get married to the love of my life. Later, I found myself in the police academy, wondering what in the hell did I get myself into. I felt like a square peg in a round hole, and didn't fit in like the other young officers.

Later on, I discovered my rough childhood helped me deal with the street people better than most other cops. I knew I was no better than the people I arrested and treated people with respect.

My empathy for the homeless on the streets is something that set me apart from most other cops in the department. I was blessed with loving parents who taught me to have strong, lifelong morals and ethics.

However, I realized that if it weren't for a couple of lucky breaks growing up, I, too, could be living on the streets or doing time in jail. So, I never forgot how to listen to a victim and hold their hand after a bad call. Empathy was an important asset of mine, but it also took its emotional toll on me.

After five years in the department, I tested for the K-9 Unit because it sounded fun to work with a dog, handling just the hot calls throughout the city. I got the K-9 position and unexpectedly found myself in the Bomb Squad as well. That job was something I didn't plan on. Only a nut plays with bombs, I thought.

One of the older patrol sergeants once described me as an aggressive K-9 handler who loved his job more than any other cop in the department. Using a police dog to search for a hidden suspect is one of the most hazardous things a cop can do. Working for two decades in the K-9 Unit was not very common because the job was so dangerous.

Constant awareness of the real chance of being hurt or killed each night took its toll. In this book I will explain the unexpected aftermath of going on thousands of high risk-calls and conducting searches for suspects who had just committed a variety of violent crimes.

I stayed in the K-9 Unit and Bomb Squad for twenty years. An adrenalin addiction soon became my main problem. I looked forward to going to work with my police dog, and the excitement of never knowing what calls I would be dispatched to. I had the freedom to patrol anywhere in the city, anytime I wanted throughout the night.

Going code three (lights and siren activated) to emergency calls was a nightly occurrence. I loved being the lead car following directly behind a suspect vehicle in a high-speed pursuit. This was the common practice in the K-9 Unit because the dogs could have a clear line of sight at the suspects when they eventually crashed and ran from a car that was usually stolen.

Being the lead car also prevented the dogs from running past other cops who were on foot, preventing a possible accidental bite of an officer, which occurred from time to time.

Rookie cops loved to run after suspects even though a police dog was in the pursuit. They usually did this only once.

The K-9 Unit was a great job for a young cop who wanted to go to all the hot calls. This went on for years. I conducted thousands of K-9 searches, hundreds of vehicle pursuits, and numerous felony arrests of all kinds.

I was involved in three separate officer involved shootings, as well as ending up in the emergency ward six times by ambulance for injuries I received in the field. All of these activities contributed to serious problems I developed over the years.

Working in such an intense unit for so many years had a deep and lasting effect on my family and me. Hypervigilance was a lifesaver on duty, but caused many personal problems at home.

Alcoholism, PTSD, suicidal thoughts, divorce, and the death of my partner were all things I didn't plan on when I became a cop. I slowly became emotionally resilient and learned to use my own experiences to help other cops.

After I left the K-9 Unit, I started teaching other cops about the unseen hazards of the job. This continued until my retirement when I then received the toughest assignment of my life.

My mom fell and broke her arm right after I retired. She needed help and had to have surgery for the nasty break. For the next six years, I took care of her every need. I fixed her meals and later had to dress her each day.

She slowly faded away with dementia and several other ailments, while I took care of her at home. I did in-home hospice care at the end of her life. It was not easy to watch my mom slowly die and changed me in many ways those last months.

I didn't want any help taking care of her from family or friends, and felt it was my duty to be by her side. She slept most of the time towards the end, giving me time to reflect on my own life.

After my mom died, I felt an overwhelming need to have some kind of purpose in life, other than playing golf. Taking care of her took up all my time and attention. Losing her left me with nothing of value to do.

I needed to pay it forward in life and decided to write this book. In the last few chapters of this book, I talk about some of the things I have learned. I talk about racism in police work as well as giving advice to young cops.

While I was taking care of my mom, I had a moment of clarity, a feeling of self-actualization. I know all living things are connected to each other in some way.

Death is not the end of the energy source contained inside us all. Our mortal bodies will come and go countless times, but our souls will live on for eternity.

## Dedication
## Goodbye, Old Friend

The first thing they taught me In school was how to use a big fat pencil. I used you throughout my school years and adult life. What a marvelous tool you were. I just pressed down, and your lead scratch marks told my story. How easy and fun you were to use.

You laid out everything on paper that I could imagine, from the most detailed mathematical problem to the beauty of a poem. You seemed to have a mind of your own, scribbling words down faster than I could think of them.

You were an extension of my mind's eye. The words seemed to flow from my brain, through my hand, and into your wooden body, which then worked its magic. What a magnificent thing to use each day and to have as a friend.

Now that I grow old, I see the growth of technology in every aspect of life. Hell, even cars park themselves nowadays. Computers in grade schools are now taking the place of my old friend the pencil. I assume the new generation will grow up learning things from the stroke of a keyboard.

My friend, the pencil may not have a spell check, but it does make you think on your own. There is a certain beauty in the simplicity of a pencil. I fear technology has made us all a little lazier in our busy lives.

Nothing in life stays the same for long. I suppose the pencil has seen its better days. From President Lincoln's great speeches that he wrote with a pencil and a piece of paper, to the simple game of tic-tac-toe, my friend the pencil was there to see them all come and go.

It's sad to see my old friend being replaced by a computer. *Out with the old and in with the new* always stung my ears with the realization that my time of replacement was also imminent.

Yes, the pencil is just an example of my generation's simple grandeur. I say thank you to the pencil for being there when I needed you. From the love letters I wrote to my last will and testament, I owe you a lifetime of gratitude.

## Introduction

What was it like to wear a badge for three decades in Sacramento, California? I have tried my best to describe my career working as a street cop. From the Police Academy to my retirement, I will share the good, the bad, and the ugly truth about police work.

I was a Sacramento police officer for thirty years. For twenty of those years, I worked in the Department's K-9 Unit and Bomb Squad. My preferred shift was from 7 pm to 5 am, because that's when the best calls came out.

I witnessed a lot of bad things during my late-night shift and was involved in countless critical incidents, including the on-duty deaths of several friends. On one occasion, I became filled with hate and anger after the senseless murder of a fellow officer and friend who was shot by a wanted parolee during a traffic stop.

That night I kept thinking I would wake up from a bad dream only to find myself still looking for the suspect who was hiding close by. I hoped I'd have the restraint not to execute the guy once my police dog found him.

Searching alongside the SWAT team that night is something I still think about. Every detail of the arrest is embedded in my mind like impressions in wet cement. Some things in my career can never be forgotten, no matter how much I wish they could.

Some of the horrible things I saw defied imagination. I arrested some really bad people who viciously attacked innocent victims of all ages. The hard-core criminals had no remorse or regrets for their actions. This only gave me more motivation to catch those truly cruel individuals. It's funny how some suspects seemed to resist arrest more than others.

This collection of true street stories will describe moments of extreme fear, excitement, and sadness I experienced along the way. No two shifts were ever the same. That's what made the job so fun. An up-front account of what it was like to laugh or cry after a radio call will teach readers what cops go through.

Some realities can never be replicated in a class and are best learned from reading the words of someone who has actually lived through what they have written about.

I want the public to hear and understand what I felt and endured during some of the calls I went on late at night. My most important qualifications to write this book are my real-life experiences working as a street cop.

One chief reason I'm writing this book is to let the public know who police officers really are. The public has seen a thousand police shoot-outs on TV; however, officer-involved shootings are actually rare events for most cops.

The vast majority of people have had minimal personal contact with the police. When they have had encounters, it's almost always related to a bad experience. Either they were crime victims, involved in a car accident, or got a ticket. The public has little awareness of what a cop's life is all about, but the stories I'll share will provide fresh insights.

People can only use their imagination to understand the fear of being shot at or the humiliation of being spit on. From my dumb rookie mistakes to the split-second decision to take a human life, each of my stories will tell the reader exactly what occurred.

Almost all cops receive physical injuries during their career, and they typically range from a bump on the head during an insignificant car crash to a bloody nose received in a fight. Hospital emergency rooms are used to treating police officers for minor injuries sustained during their shift. Cops often need a few stitches or some X-rays, and are then released that same day.

Sadly, the same number of officers are also mentally injured during their career. No cop can work the streets for very long before they encounter some really bad things. Words alone cannot describe the shock police officers may experience when they first view the horrific images of a gruesome accident or a crime scene.

Some ugly aspects of being a cop will never change. Seeing the body of a small child who just drowned in a backyard pool is something that I will never forget. And how do you comfort a grieving parent who just lost their child to an apparently senseless suicide?

Cops also must become good listeners and show genuine compassion for people in their time of need. This is something the public doesn't see on the nightly news or read about in the morning paper.

Many officers who have small children of their own at home have a very hard time with certain calls. Any veteran cop knows bad calls involving children happen from time to time, leaving them asking "Why?" Why does a husband kill his wife and then his two small children during a domestic disturbance call, while you're on the inner perimeter of the residence?

I can still hear the gunshots followed by the children screaming and then being ordered by the Patrol Watch Commander to stand by and wait for the SWAT team to arrive.

I'll always carry the burden of heavy guilt for not making an immediate entry into the residence. Disobeying a direct order by the watch commander and making an entry on my own would have cost me my job, but I might have saved the children's lives.

The public would be surprised at the mental toll police work takes on some officers. PTSD, alcoholism, and hypervigilance are perils of the job that young officers need to be aware of.

Most cops know deep down inside when they need to talk to someone after a bad call. But many would rather talk with another cop than with a trained mental health professional. Some cops can talk to their spouse or a close friend, while others reach out to their church for assistance.

I kept things bottled up and desperately avoided anything that reminded me of the bad things I saw and experienced. I never talked to anyone about the intense flashbacks from one incident. Once the flashback or "movie" started playing in my head, nothing could stop it until it completely played out. The flashbacks slowly drove me crazy.

Like countless other people, I turned to alcohol to self-medicate myself. After a twenty-nine year marriage, during my divorce I drank heavily one night and had suicidal thoughts. The sad fact is many cops still struggle with the stigma of seeking help from a mental health professional.

In this book, I openly describe my PTSD that I acquired after several critical incidents. I still occasionally have bad thoughts and see hideous images that I replay in my mind.

I hope to offer readers a better understanding of the cumulative psychological effects of critical incidents and the potential emotional damage done to officers over the course of their career.

Yet the negative stigma of asking for help has continued to profoundly impact professional police work as well as officers' personal lives. Every law enforcement agency needs to address these critical mental health issues and needs through enhanced training and support.

Fighting the stigma of asking for help has always been an uphill battle in law enforcement. Unfortunately, there are many reasons why police officers don't get the specialized help they need after being involved in a critical incident. Police officers don't want to get a "jacket" or a reputation of being mentally weak or unstable. Cops often think seeing a therapist will hurt their chances of promotion or transferring to another unit. The end result is most cops don't seek any professional help at all.

In order to survive the job, police officers need to become emotionally resilient to the extreme events they come in contact with. The cumulative effect on going to scores of suicides, homicides, and horrible car accidents can be devastating. Thus, knowing how to protect your mind is just as important as wearing your bullet-proof vest.

Substance abuse, divorce, and suicide are all extreme risks of the job that no rookie officer ever expects will happen to them. Many common problems of the job such as hypervigilance, depression, and family difficulties, can be substantially mitigated by understanding the causes and learning stress reduction techniques.

I have provided important advice to young and old officers alike on how to deal with the invisible dangers of the job. The recommendations may save their marriages or even their lives.

Although cops may develop the needed emotional resiliency to handle the bloody crime scenes, horrible car wrecks and awful suicides, even the most hardened veteran officers can be traumatized by some calls.

Police work may still take its toll on psychologically fit officers in the department. Some bad calls stay with cops forever, just like our combat veterans who continue to feel the pain of a friend's death that occurred many years ago.

Readers will learn about the negative effects of seeing homeless people living in the streets in the worst living conditions imaginable. Most cops learn to become detached from their own emotions in response to these experiences. However, I never became cold and unsympathetic toward the street people I often saw sleeping in dirty alleys.

Witnessing people living in subhuman conditions had a lasting effect on me, because I knew they all had their own stories to tell. Police officers should withhold moral judgments and never think they are better than the drunk lying in the gutter. They have not walked in their shoes, if they are wearing any at all.

Bad things happen to good people, and the continuum of good to bad morality cuts across all segments of society. Many cops pay a heavy price if they're not mindful of the inherent dangers of the job.

Going home alive after your shift is over is the most important lesson an officer must learn. To all the young cops, please always think of your family first and the job second. You will live a longer and happier life.

People need to recognize that the vast majority of police officers throughout the country are good people. Recently "Law Enforcement" has been painted with the broad brush of systemic racism.

Police officers throughout the country are routinely portrayed as the "enemy" through negative national press and ongoing media coverage detailing alleged abuses and tragic incidents.

This is a very sad thing to witness for an old, retired cop who loved his job. Police officers typically receive little thanks for doing a dangerous job each day protecting the public. It's my intention to give voice to the belief that police work is still an honorable profession.

## Chapter 1
## My Lost Childhood

I had many childhood friends that died violent deaths. Being killed in a car crash or going to prison was a common occurrence in our small town. I am sure I would have followed in their paths if I hadn't become a cop. I grew up as a happy kid in Northern California, but my childhood ended much too soon.

My older brother, Billy, only dreamed of becoming a professional baseball player. He would have made it into the big leagues, if he was three seconds faster in the forty-yard dash.

I was a big tattletale growing up. Since I often snitched on my brother, I got my share of backroom beatings from him when our dad wasn't home. Using me as a human piñata was his favorite way of getting his baseball practice in for the day. Billy also had a great imagination. He often used medieval methods of torturing me.

Most of Billy's pranks were innocent, but sometimes he went too far. Like the time he made me eat an oleander pod. Our father was a lab technician and knew that I had to vomit the poisonous plant up immediately. He made me drink several glasses of warm salt water, which did the trick. I was traumatized for life and never liked vegetables after that.

One time, Billy told me to stick my finger in an empty light bulb socket. Being the obedient little brother, I did what I was told. Then Billy turned on the light switch. I lit up like a human Christmas tree. You could have heard my scream several miles away.

On another occasion of sibling torture, Billy told me to stick my head in an air vent at the bottom of our garage's rear wall. He told me he'd climbed through the vent the day before. My brother explained his technique. He said if I could get my head through the vent, then my entire body could squeeze through. I was never the smartest kid on the block and believed my brother much too often.

Billy left for school, and I stayed home because I was not of school age yet. My mom was singing while vacuuming the house when I tried to crawl through the vent. It only took a few seconds for me to get my head stuck. My cries for help went unnoticed for thirty minutes because mom could not hear me. She later said she thought she heard a cat crying when she was vacuuming. Mom went outside to look for the poor cat, only to find my head wedged in the vent and my little body trying to get free.

She used a bar of soap for lubrication and pulled my head out of the vent, ripping part of my scalp off. Needless to say, Billy got a good spanking with a belt when our dad got home. We only got a few spankings like that growing up because it didn't take long to learn they hurt like hell.

I took my lumps from Billy for years. One day I tried to get even and almost killed him. I just got a brand-new Schwinn "Stingray" bicycle for my birthday. The single speed bike had a banana seat, butterfly handlebars, and a coaster brake on the rear tire sprocket. The bike was the envy of every kid on the block, including my jealous brother, who didn't have one yet.

One hot summer evening, we were doing spinouts on my bike in our driveway. A spinout is when you raise your foot up and slam on the rear brake, spinning the rear of the bike in a half circle. We were racing as fast as we could from across the street towards the front of our house. At the last second, we would do a spinout, seeing how close we could come to the front wall. When *Gilligan's Island* came on TV, Billy threw my bike down and said it was his turn when he came back out.

I was no angel at that time in my life. I'd had enough of his bullying and thought it was time to get even with my brother, once and for all. It only took me a few seconds to remove the bike's rear coaster brake.

When Billy came back outside, he grabbed the bike and raced off across the street. He was standing up, pedaling as fast as he could go, when he tried to slam on the brake. He was only a few feet from the wall and was going at least twenty-five miles per hour when he tried to stop. I will never forget the look of surprise on his face just before he slammed into the wall.

The collision of his body hitting our house sounded like a sonic boom. Our living room windows shook from the crash. The sudden impact knocked Billy out cold. Our dad heard the loud noise and ran outside, finding Billy lying motionless.

Dad picked Billy up to take him to the hospital, then asked me what happened. Being an honest, truthful kid, I said I didn't know what happened. "He just wrecked."

Billy was taken to the hospital emergency room and received seven stitches above his left eye and had a slight concussion. I replaced the coaster brake in a few seconds as soon as they left.

I never told my dad how the accident happened, and I didn't tell Billy the truth for twenty-five years. I never thought he would get hurt that badly. Billy's front tooth was chipped, and he got a big scar from the incident. I finally got my revenge that day.

Billy's beatings made me a very tough kid. I didn't take any shit from friends growing up. I didn't like to fight, but I wasn't scared to square off.

Later on, when I was sixteen years old, I hung around with a rough crowd of older guys who liked to look for fights every weekend after we got drunk. One hot summer night, I was going to go out to the county fair with one of my friends, Rick.

He wasn't big or strong, but he was passionate about fighting. He didn't lose many fights because he had a lot of experience growing up battling with his three older brothers, who loved to pick on him.

On this rare occasion, I had a date with a girl, as I was never the ladies' man. I took my date to dinner and a show, but still didn't get very far with her. I phoned Rick the next morning to see how much fun he had at the fair.

Rick's sister answered the phone, and it was obvious she had just been crying. She explained that Rick had gotten into a fight with a guy at the fair. He was drunk and beat the shit out of the dude, as usual.

As the man was driving away in a car, Rick had to throw one more punch. He reached through the front passenger window and punched the guy in the face. To Rick's surprise, the guy came up with a twenty-five-caliber handgun and shot him once in the chest. Rick died at the hospital several hours later.

I never liked to fight because being punched in the nose hurt like hell. It didn't take me long to figure out it was more fun to get high and drink with the girls than hang around with the guys.

I never went all the way with any high school girls, but in my junior year, I got an "A" from my friend's older sister. She was home from college and taught me things for the first time. I was a fast learner in that new subject matter.

Living across the street from a school ground provided me with the biggest front yard any kid could have. I played many years of sandlot tackle football growing up. We also played hundreds of basketball and baseball games in that schoolyard. My favorite game was baseball.

I started first string in three sports during my freshman year in high school. I couldn't afford to get in trouble with the law or I would be kicked off the teams. I was a pretty good football and baseball player, and played both sports all four years. After that, I played ten years of organized baseball in various different leagues.

Being active in sports was always a big part of my life. I learned very important lessons from the many coaches that I admired. I will always happily remember many of my teammates of all colors for the rest of my life. My coaches were colorblind to a player's race. They only wanted the fastest and toughest kid for any given position. I knew the coaches all had their own personal thoughts on different cultures, but they kept them to themselves.

Cops are the same way, or at least we should be. They should also always keep their personal opinion or attitude to themselves when it comes to controversial issues like abortion, religion, or gay rights.

\*\*\*

My mom was the nicest person in the world, who never drank, smoked, or cursed in her life. She always went to church on Sundays and had the prettiest voice in the church choir. It's sad to say our mom had little control over us and we were often rude to her.

One day Dad bought Mom a new typewriter. Playing around, he typed his Last Will and Testament. As usual, he wrote something funny. He left everything to our family cat Boots and Jimmy. Jimmy was our seventeen-year-old severely mentally handicapped next-door neighbor.

Early the next morning, I heard my dad use the bathroom. Then came a loud noise and my mother's scream from my parent's room. When

I rushed in, my dad was having a massive heart attack, which lasted for several minutes.

I ordered Mom out of the room and told her to call for an ambulance because I had to start CPR on my father. He had stopped breathing and had no pulse. It was as if I was having a bad dream and would soon wake up.

After several minutes of giving mouth to mouth breathing and a great number of chest compressions, a strange thing occurred. My dad bolted upright only for a second and said, "Take care of your mom." He then collapsed and stopped breathing for the last time.

I was only sixteen, but I can still remember how my childhood vanished that morning. The weight of taking care of my mother was now on my shoulders for life.

I started dating my future wife while we were in college together. We were soon talking about marriage, and I knew I would need a good paying job. My mother told me she would look in the paper for a job. A few days, later she told me about an opening for a Sacramento City police officer.

I laughed at the idea of being a cop because I was used to running from them as a teenager for various minor offenses. I gave it some thought though, and knew I had to have a good job if I wanted to get married. Plus, it sounded like it might be a fun job.

1964, from the left, Mike's brother Bill holding his cat, Shadow. Mike's father holding their dog, Joe. Mike's mother holding Mike's cat, Pork Chops.

When Mike was very young, he asked his mom what they were having for dinner. She replied, "pork chops." Mike screamed in terror and began to cry at the thought of them eating his cat for dinner.

## Chapter 2
## The Testing Procedure

I took the written test along with twenty-five hundred other applicants. I thought I didn't have a snowball's chance in hell to pass, as I was not good at taking tests. Luckily for me, the test was only pass or fail. I passed and went to the next testing stage.

At the oral interview, several people sitting at a table fired a variety of hypothetical questions at me. I was lucky because I scored one hundred percent on my first oral board.

The next test was a five-hour-long written psychological test, which left me feeling like a firebug. To my relief, I passed that test as well. Fortunately, in 1977 there was no polygraph test administered as part of the testing procedure, because I sometimes still smoked marijuana.

The last part of the hiring process was the chief's interview. I heard that the chief would just ask me some simple questions, to find out what type of person I was. I thought this was just a preliminary talk before I got the job.

For some reason, I was extremely nervous waiting outside the chief's office for my turn. Once I entered his office, I became twice as nervous, and felt like I was going to puke on him. His face looked like it went through a meat grinder at some point in his life. The room was filled with heavy cigarette smoke, because the chief was a chain smoker.

He didn't look up once or offer to shake my hand. The chief told me to sit down while he looked over my paperwork. He asked about my family and other seemingly innocent questions. I thought I had the job in the bag, as this interview was the easiest of all the testing procedures I had gone through.

Then the chief looked up at me for the first time. I thought the interview was almost over. Out of the blue, he asked if I ever smoked marijuana. After almost shitting down both my legs, I took a deep breath and said yes.

Thinking I should have said no, I thought they would never hire me.

Then the old bastard asked me to tell him about the time I smoked marijuana. Thinking as fast as I could on my feet, I made up some innocent sounding story about my brother offering me some pot on Christmas Eve when he came home from college. We shared a joint in our backyard.

I couldn't believe my ears when he asked me if there were any other times. I took a breath and said yes. That sadistic old fart then asked me to tell him about that time.

Again, I made up some naïve sounding story. I told him my senior high school football team had a party after we won our championship. Some of the guys were passing a joint around, and I took a few puffs.

The chief then asked me one more question that may have gotten me the job. He looked me straight in the eyes and asked if there were any other times I smoked pot. I didn't blink an eye, stared right back at him, and said, "Yes, there were other times."

I walked out of the department and headed for the first bar, because I knew I had just blown that interview. I knew the chief wasn't going to hire a pot head. When I received a letter from the department the next week, I didn't want to open it and have to tell my mom that I didn't get the job.

To my surprise, I ranked number two, out of twenty-five hundred other people. My mom was the proudest lady alive. She always was suspicious about me cheating because I wasn't very book smart.

Today the testing procedure is a little different. The hiring process has several stages designed to identify and disqualify any racist police candidates, including a one-year probationary period where the applicant can be fired without cause. Any signs of racism detected during the extensive hiring process would be an automatic cause of dismissal.

The first thing in the hiring process of all applicants is a comprehensive background investigation. Highly trained background investigators examine school records and employment history, then conduct personal interviews with each prospective police candidate.

One of the background investigator's primary jobs is looking for any reports or signs of racial biases or tendencies. If the police candidate passes their background investigation, they will then take an extensive written psychological test.

## Chapter 3
## The Police Academy

After I was hired, I had to go to a sixteen-week police academy at the new California Highway Patrol (CHP) Academy. It was a live-in school, which was recognized as one of the best modern police academies in the country, if not the world. I found it difficult to room with a stranger, but some of the other students in the class turned out to be lifelong friends of mine.

I soon learned to be "seen" and not "heard" while in the academy. The instructors ordered us around like children.

We were told, if we can't handle the pressure in the academy, we won't be able to handle working the streets.

The first day I wanted to punch one of the instructors out. He screamed at a female student for being late for class. She started to cry, and the instructor gave her a bad time in front of the class. *What an asshole,* I thought.

The first week I wondered if I made a mistake taking the job, because I didn't seem to fit in. I had to study twice as hard as the other students, because my brain was pickled from drinking so much beer. I was very intimidated by being around a bunch of instructors that acted like Marine drill sergeants.

It was hard for me to get used to the idea of being a cop, because I grew up as a little juvenile delinquent. As a young kid, I never thought about how dangerous being a cop might be. In one of my first Officer Safety classes, I learned the details of the deadly Newhall CHP shooting. Hearing how one of the suspects viciously executed a defenseless CHP officer, as he was trying to reload his empty gun, left a lasting impression on me.

During that famous traffic stop on April 5, 1970, four officers were killed. None of them carried speed reloaders, and the shotgun was at port-arms position. None of the officers wore vests, and they failed to wait for backup, which was only minutes away.

I will never forget one particular class in the police academy, because of the instructor's brilliant performance. This instructor taught a courtroom testimony class, but his name was not on the schedule to teach. He showed up ten minutes late to class, wearing a T-shirt and jeans.

The guy was a district attorney investigator. He told the class his boss informed him at the last damn minute that he had to teach at the academy. It was obvious the instructor was not happy about the late request.

He continued to rant on about being asked to teach with no notice. He then said he didn't want to be there teaching a bunch of dumb rookies.

After taking several minutes of verbal abuse from this jerk, one of our more outspoken students raised his hand.

This student was a little older than the rest of us. He was a Vietnam combat veteran who had killed more than his share of people in the war. The instructor said, "Now, what do you want?" The student told the instructor he thought he was an asshole for talking to the class so unprofessionally. For a few seconds you could have heard a pin drop. It was so quiet.

The instructor then flew into a rage and ordered the student to step outside the classroom. We all thought that they were going outside to fight. After several minutes, the academy sergeant walked into the classroom.

We all thought we had seen the last of our fellow classmate because of his behavior. The same student then walked in and took his seat. Neither the sergeant nor the student said a word.

All of us felt the tension in the classroom. The same instructor then walked into the classroom. Now he was dressed in a suit and tie. We soon learned the instructor was just acting in order to make a point of the importance of first impressions.

I was completely fooled and a little scared by his performance. He continued to teach the class, which turned out to be one of the best classes we had during the entire academy.

The instructor was a hell of a nice guy, with a great sense of humor. Nothing happened to the student who spoke out. We always respected him for speaking up for the class.

Three months after he taught the class at the academy, our instructor and another investigator attempted to serve a simple misdemeanor warrant at a residence. The suspect was only wanted for a minor crime.

As the two investigators were walking up the residential driveway, the suspect appeared out of nowhere, holding a rifle. The suspect shot both investigators, killing our instructor. The other investigator lived, and the suspect went to prison. This was my first, but unfortunately not my last time, that a cop I knew lost his life in the line of duty.

After I graduated from the academy, I never forgot about the instructor who was killed. Our instructor taught the class not to judge a book by its cover. His last lesson was to approach all calls with caution.

I always remembered how much the instructor enjoyed teaching our class. He was a great actor who was good at instructing young officers. He had us in the palm of his hands and fooled everyone.

Later in my career, teaching was a big part of my job. I always tried to have fun, even though public speaking can be hard.

Teaching officers about K-9 patrol tactics, bombs, and explosives kept me busy. I always tried my best to make classes fun for the students, because If they liked the class, they would be more likely to retain the valuable information that was provided.

Mike's Basic Police academy class "79BR2." It was a 12-week, live-in academy held at the CHP academy in West Sacramento, California. The Highway Patrol academy was and still is considered one of the best police training facilities in the nation, if not the world.

## Chapter 4
## My Rookie Years

Graduating from the police academy was just the beginning of the ride of my life. I had no idea what was in store for me. That first year was filled with fear, excitement, and extreme apprehension of being a cop.

I had a rough time during my probationary period and almost washed out. Learning all the various codes, rules and regulations was hard for me since I was not very book smart.

It felt strange wearing a police uniform in public. Being nervous on my first day at work was an understatement. Not that long ago I was running from the cops, and now I wore a badge.

The older cops had several stripes sewn on their sleeves, each standing for five years of service on the department. Most of them just smiled, but didn't say too much to me. They all knew I was a brand-new rookie officer, who didn't know how to be a real street cop.

I didn't want to look the watch commander in the eyes as we passed each other in the hallway on my first day. He was a former United States Marine who enjoyed intimidating young cops just out of the Academy.

The patrol division roll call room was filled with cigar and cigarette smoke and about fifty uniformed swing shift officers. Back then, roll calls were something we looked forward to attending, because they were damn funny. Before roll call started, the older cops would start telling stories that made the supervisors shake their heads and walk out of the room.

They used extremely foul language, even though there were three females police officers in the room. Back then, the few female cops in our department didn't make complaints against male officers for using bad language.

Roll call consisted of a sergeant standing at the front of the roll call room, then calling everyone's name and telling them what unit they were assigned to work. The sergeant would then relay important information relating to the prior shift's activity and about any new crime series or wanted subjects.

Things slowly changed at roll calls over the years. Smoking inside the building was banned in the early 1980s. One time a female officer made a complaint about the foul language at a roll call. After that, each supervisor was warned to stop letting officers tell offensive stories before roll call and not to use vulgar language. Roll calls changed when cops could not tell raunchy jokes and offend female officers.

## Chapter 5
## My First Field Training Officer

During my first year in the police department, I had to complete a very long six-month probationary period. During that time, I could be terminated without cause or reason. All rookie officers were trained by different FTOs (Field Training Officers) who wrote daily and weekly performance evaluations.

Trainees had to meet the minimum performance requirements, or they would be washed out or fired. Some of my training officers were real pricks with obvious control issues. I was told to lie low during my probation and not get into any trouble, advice I gladly took.

Most of my old FTOs didn't want to hear what the other FTOs were teaching. It was their car, and I had to do as they said. Back then, a rookie didn't talk back or make excuses for mistakes.

Being seen and not heard was my motto. A few of my FTOs were Vietnam War veterans who had just gotten out of the service after seeing the horrors of combat. It was apparent some of them were a little crazy and might kick your ass if you got smart with them. They were good cops who didn't take shit from anyone on the streets.

After roll call, my first FTO introduced himself and we walked to the parking lot to pick up a "Black and White" patrol car. As we sat in the car, he gave his regular, first night safety talk.

He made it clear that rookie cops can always learn the different codes or how to write a report, but officer safety is the most important thing that must be learned from day one. He also instructed me to always know my location in case we needed to call for help.

I was then shown how to check out a patrol car before each shift. We turned on all the emergency lights and the siren to make sure everything worked. The back seat was searched to make sure there was no leftover evidence, weapons, or contraband from the previous shift.

Believe it or not, my FTO told me he once found a loaded gun under the rear seat of a patrol car he was checking before one shift. He later found out that a robbery suspect hid the gun under the seat after his arrest.

The officer who previously used the car missed the gun when he searched the suspect. He had also failed to search the back seat of his patrol car after removing the culprit at the jail. Fortunately, his supervisor liked him, so he only received a well-deserved documented counseling.

I was taught to "always" check the rear seat of the patrol car after anyone was in it. This included anyone I provided a ride for. This way, if I ever found any drugs or contraband after a suspect was removed from my car, I could testify in court it had to be theirs, because I was trained to always check my rear seat after anyone was removed from it.

Next was checking the twelve-gauge shotgun that was kept in the patrol car. My training officer said to make sure the gun was empty, and then look inside the barrel to check for any gum wrappers or cigarette ashes.

My first FTO was my favorite and later became a lifetime friend. I learned he was a Vietnam veteran who did two tours with a Special Forces Unit. He told me how he survived for days in the jungle, and sad stories about the friends he lost.

I got to know my training officer pretty well while riding with him for a month. I learned a lot of valuable lessons by just watching how he treated each individual he interacted with during our shift.

My FTO told me not to take anything people say or do personally. He said people just see the uniform and the badge, but not the person wearing them. Cops represent authority, which many people automatically dislike for various reasons of their own.

I was told to develop my own style of police work and how to talk to people. Soon I felt more comfortable interacting with the drug dealers, gang members, and other street people than the supervisors I worked for.

A cop must learn to be an actor and have a flexible demeanor with each person. I was trained to respect and treat all people fairly, no matter what my personal feelings were.

I learned early on that no two shifts were the same, and never to let my guard down. Even on routine calls, I was taught to expect the unexpected. If my life was in danger, there was no such thing as a fair fight. I was advised not to wrestle with suspects on the ground. If needed, I should use a brick, rock, or anything else in order to stay alive during a fight.

Parolees may be nice to me, but I should never turn my back on them because they will kill in a split second in order to get away. A parolee once told me after fighting with him over a gun in his coat pocket, "Business is business. Nothing personal."

Most of my other FTOs told me to forget the academy crap and watch and learn from the older officers. They were right, of course. The Police Academy taught me the essential bookwork that I needed to know, but my Field

Training Officers taught me how to stay alive while working on the streets.

I was a young cop, that was captivated by the "awe" of police work my first year in the department. Each shift was an adventure, because I had no idea what was coming on the next radio call. I think that's what made the job so much fun.

Seeing my first murder victim and fatal car wreck left me with a sense of how fragile and unfair life can be. After a few years in the department, I got used to seeing dead bodies, however I could never get used to seeing a small dead child. I don't think any cop can. That is one of the unfortunate things in police work that will never change.

I struggled with report writing and remembering all the codes and regulations during my first year of training, however, I always felt at ease talking with criminals, such as parolees and people on probation.

I still felt I had more in common with the people I arrested than with the cops I was working around. It was hard for me to get used to people staring at me in my uniform when I was eating at restaurants.

Being a young, impressionable rookie cop, I learned more than I should have from the old timers. I was very lucky some of the practical jokes I learned from them didn't get me fired.

I also learned how to administer street justice during some arrests. Sometimes I got a little carried away when arresting a child molester, rapist, or other very bad people. A well written report saved my ass more than once.

Our after-hours drinking was common knowledge to the Watch Commander and other supervisors. They must have thought it was important for us to relax and get things off our chest, because they always looked the other way when they drove by. They had all done the same thing when they were young cops.

## Chapter 6
## Choir Practice

Getting things off your chest after drinking more than one beer was something we all did from time to time. Telling your friends about fighting a crazy giant who tried to take your gun away is an example of the things cops want to talk about after their shift is over.

The fact is, all cops get the hell scared out of them from time to time, and feel the need to talk to another cop about a bad call. Cops can't go home and talk to their family about seeing a decomposed dead body. At times, only another police officer can understand what it's like to be a cop.

Drinking beer was part of my life growing up, and I soon learned what choir practice was. A retired LAPD Officer, by the name of Joseph Wambaugh, became a famous author. One of his first books, *The Choirboys*, talked about a group of cops that drank together in a city park after their shift was over. They called their nightly drunken parties choir practice.

I attended many choir practices during my first year working as a patrol officer. For the first several years on the job, it was common practice for me and other cops to stand around a barrel of burning wood and drink beer and tell stories in the police department's parking lot until the sun came up.

It was a way of relaxing and venting our many frustrations about the radio calls we handled that night, and listening to some very sad calls we all experienced from time to time.

We learned from the old-time cops that we really were angels compared to what cops were like in the 1950s and 1960s. The public has no idea what the cops got away with back then. Use of force issues were a joke unless you killed someone.

Even if a cop killed someone, little investigation would be started unless there were witnesses. The cops always seemed to be standing too far away to hear a conversation that ended up as a complaint against another officer. Cops used to have "selective hearing" when it was necessary to protect another cop.

Hearing the old-time cops telling their war stories was something straight out of Hollywood. I heard stories about "Police Bag Men" who accepted money from the pimps not to hassle their girls.

This was not an uncommon practice in the 1940s and 1950s. The old cops who walked the foot-beat often had more than a few drinks during their shift. Some got so drunk they could barely make it back to the station.

Our parties were getting bigger, and we were getting home later each night. My wife complained and warned me of the potential chance for an arrest for DUI. I lived in the city and thought as long as I didn't get into an accident, no fellow cop in the department would arrest me.

Back then, if a cop was pulled over for drunk driving in the city, he would just get a mandatory ride home. Arresting another cop, who worked in the same department, for a misdemeanor DUI was unheard of years ago.

Our parties went on for years until one night an old-time cop invited a "cop groupie" to one of our tailgaters. Things soon got carried away. Most of the cops were happily married, faithful husbands.

Several of the married cops were sexually gratified in the back of the old timer's 1979 Dodge van, by the sixty-five-year-old alcoholic. Three days later she made an internal affairs complaint after she was arrested for being drunk in public.

She stated ten young cops got her drunk and forced her to orally copulate with them. Well, needless to say that ended the after-hours drinking escapades for me and several others.

## Chapter 7
## The Jacket You Can't Take Off

I started to have a drinking problem as a teenager. I liked the effects of alcohol and getting a buzz on the weekends. There wasn't a lot else to do while growing up in a small town.

Attending every party after my high school football games led to me becoming a very young alcoholic. I was never arrested because of my drinking, but I came close several times. Running from the police saved me from going to jail on more than one occasion.

I never drank on duty as a cop; however, I made up for it on my days off. Drinking beer during most of my meals was a habit I picked up in college. Having a few beers with my pizza or steak was a normal thing.

I rarely drank more than four or five beers at any one time, because that was above my normal limit. I liked to maintain a nice warm feeling of slight intoxication throughout the day.

Drinking more than that usually resulted in me doing or saying something stupid, resulting in an argument with my wife. One of my biggest regrets in life was drinking beer in front of our two girls while they were growing up. I was a horrible role model for my kids.

When my wife and I went to the many police parties and various functions over the years, I was not shy about having a good time. I wasn't a loud drunk, and I didn't make any scenes, but it was easy to tell I liked to tip a few.

I soon got my well-deserved reputation for being a heavy drinker. When a cop gets a reputation of being a drunk, he gets what's called a "jacket". Once you get a jacket for drinking, it's something you can't take off, even if you become a sober drunk.

About a month after I stopped drinking, I attended the K-9 comedy night charity function held at a local comedy club. This was one big party, where cops let their hair down and had a good time after having more than a few drinks.

I had several glasses of orange juice, minus the vodka, but still had a great time. The next day a female officer, who I didn't know very well, started talking about the show. She then surprised me by saying how wasted I looked. She probably wouldn't have believed me if I told her I was stone sober.

## Chapter 8
## Old Timers

Many of the older cops were quite the characters. The young cops were amused by listening to their stories for hours on end. Sometimes we didn't get home until the sun came up, which made our wives very unhappy. One of the older cops was on my first patrol team. Bob was the nicest cop, and everyone in the department liked him. He was also a great storyteller.

Our captain, who was a former Marine, would always have a uniform inspection once a month before roll call. Our shoes and leather gear had to be cleaned and shined. During the inspection, we would all stand at attention, while the old captain walked up and down each line, inspecting each of the officers.

Each officer would unload their department-issued 38 revolver, hold the bullets in one hand and a clean gun in the other. The captain wore white cotton gloves to make certain your gun was clean.

All the other cops wanted to stand next to Bob during inspection. The sloppy way he dressed, and his dirty shoes would make the guy standing next to him look great.

One inspection will always stand out in my memory. During the inspection, it was Bob's turn to unload his gun and present it to the captain. Bob opened the cylinder to his six-shot revolver, only to find it was already unloaded.

The captain then asked Bob when he last checked his weapon.

Bob was not a liar, and admitted he last checked his gun at the firing range during the last qualification shoot, which was held three weeks earlier. We all realized Bob had been covering us on numerous high risk, dangerous gun calls for the last several weeks with an unloaded gun.

Needless to say, our captain was quite pissed off and chewed Bob out in private. However, nothing else happened because he also liked Bob so much. From that incident, I learned to always check my gun before each shift to make sure it was loaded.

## Chapter 9
## Code-7

Eating, or having what cops call a Code-7 was an adventure. That was the first thing a cop would ask his partner at the beginning of their shift. "Where do you want to eat tonight?"

When I started police work in the 1970s, every good restaurant in town never charged the police for meals. Most cops would leave nice tips after eating.

Receiving free or half price meals was common practice among most of the cops when I came on. The restaurant owners were glad to show their appreciation to the patrol officers who drove by their business several times during their shift. It only took a few times being robbed for the owners to want some type of protection from the cops and liked us to come in and eat for free.

I had an old training officer that brought me to a Chinese buffet on my first night out on patrol. I loved Chinese food and ate three platefuls, when I found out that cops didn't pay for their food. The job sounded better all the time.

After dinner, my training officer and I were sitting in our patrol car talking. I was listening to the radio when I started having a hard time breathing. My training officer was amused when I complained to him about my ailment. He had trained hundreds of young officers and knew right away what my problem was. He told me to loosen the Velcro straps to my bullet-proof vest because I ate too much. Once I followed his instructions, I could breathe normally again. I was starting to understand the importance of street experience.

Things changed over the years. When I came on, every Taco Bell and McDonald's gave free food to any cop. Over time, more and more places stopped the practice.

Private restaurant owners still gave free or half-price meals to the police. It was nice to go to a Chinese or Mexican place to eat for Code-7 at least once a week.

On a couple of occasions after the owner or one of the cooks were arrested for a D.U.I., that restaurant stopped giving out free food.

Over time, police work became more professional in a lot of ways. Police departments stopped having a blind eye to gratuities of any kind, even a free hamburger.

Now days police officers bring their own food for Code-7 or pay full price when they eat in a restaurant. I am sure a few cops still find places to eat that charge half-price, but they are not the majority.

Many late-night businesses still offer free coffee to cops because the owners like to have them around, so they won't get robbed.

## Chapter 10
## My First Ticket

I still can recall the first traffic ticket I ever wrote. I was with another old training officer when I pulled over a car for a minor violation. Four gorgeous girls, in their late teens or early twenties, occupied the car. It was important to impress my new training officer with my officer safety techniques.

I held my flashlight under my left armpit, leaving my gun hand free. I then walked up to the car and stood slightly to the rear of the driver's door. This is how we were taught to conduct a traffic stop in the academy.

Things were going well until I reached for her license and registration with my left hand. I dropped my flashlight and, as luck would have it, the damn light rolled halfway under the car. I had to lie down on my stomach and reach out in order to retrieve my light. Barney Fife could have done a better job.

I returned to the squad car, only to see my training officer splitting a gut from laughing so hard. I wrote the girl a minor traffic ticket and returned to her car for her to sign the citation. She was also still laughing at me.

After she signed the citation, I attempted to tear the ticket out of my black leather ticket book. Murphy's Law was on my side that day for sure. While attempting to remove the ticket, I accidentally tore it in half.

I can still remember my training officer and the four girls in the car laughing hysterically. The driver then asked me if it was the first ticket I ever wrote. I admitted it was, and let her go with a warning because I didn't have any scotch tape. I never did write many tickets after that horrible ordeal.

## Chapter 11
## First Vehicle Pursuit

I remember my first vehicle pursuit as if it were yesterday, even though I've been involved in hundreds of chases during my career. Some pursuits ended when I ran a pedestrian over, or hit a bicyclist with my squad car; naturally, they all were accidental.

Seeing their bodies flying off the hood of my police car after they robbed or shot someone brought no tears to my face. My main concern was how to write a good report on how I hit them while they were fleeing with a gun in their hand.

I was taught to never lie in a police report. My first sergeant told me to write my true emotions during the confrontations I had, even if I had to say that I feared for my life. I put every detail of any force I used in my reports. My actions were justified to cover myself.

Cops are too macho to say they were afraid or scared during a critical incident. Understandable fear is a cop's best defense during a shooting investigation. If I ever used any force on a call, I learned how to explain my actions in my reports by describing all the little details of each departmentally approved technique that I used.

This habit of documenting details would later help me, when a grand jury report scrutinized our K-9 Unit. I was sued several times over the years and had to rely on my reports for assistance.

I finally got to be alone, with no field training officer. This was a high point in any officer's career. I now could do anything I wanted. I could eat at my favorite restaurants and go on different calls. Best of all, I didn't have to listen to a training officer tell me what to do or where to drive.

It was scary to be by myself those first few nights. Hoping I didn't make any mistake that got me in trouble or cause someone else to get hurt was always on my mind.

Our old sergeant told the new rookies to take it easy the first few weeks and just cover the older officers on calls. He also said, be careful driving. Our first night out, we were all racing to every good call that we heard being dispatched.

We were like kids in a candy shop, running red traffic lights with our police car's red and blue lights flashing, and sirens wailing away. Using our own discretion was a new thing for us, now that we worked alone.

One of our department's legends was a crime scene investigator by the name of Gale

Right, who was known for being at the right place at the right time. Our C.S.I.s were regular police officers who patrolled the streets, but also collected fingerprints and processed crime scenes.

Gale had two reputations that everyone knew about. He had wrecked more squad cars than any other cop in the history of our department. Gale also made some of the best arrests a cop could make. He was a hard worker and spent his time looking for bad guys. He did not spend his time in some coffee shop trying to pick up on a waitress, like so many other cops did.

My second night out alone turned out to be a real thriller. A radio call about an armed robbery was dispatched citywide. The suspect robbed a man and his wife at gunpoint as they left an upscale restaurant located downtown. He also took the victim's car, along with money and jewelry.

My district was five miles away from the robbery, so I thought the suspect would never come my way. My dad used to say if you want to catch fish you have to have your pole in the water. Gale always had his pole in the water when it came to looking for suspects. Gale found the car ten seconds after the call came from the dispatcher.

The strange thing was the car had already driven at least five miles away from the crime scene by the time the call was dispatched. Gale, once again, was following an armed robber by himself.

I was close by and soon pulled in behind Gale's squad car. I was scared shitless because this was the first major call without a training officer. As luck would have it, the suspect took off like a rabbit, going one hundred mph down the freeway.

Gale told me to handle the radio transmissions, while he took the lead car in the pursuit. The suspect was a well-known local parolee, with felony warrants and nothing to lose. During the fifteen-minute chase, he drove at extremely high speeds, even when we sometimes entered residential areas.

The suspect crashed his stolen car in an apartment complex and fled on foot. Gale and I chased the guy down and cornered him between two walls. The suspect raised his hands while Gale pointed his gun at his head and told him to "Get the F--K on the ground." I also drew my weapon, not knowing what to do next. This was the first time I pointed my gun at a suspect without a training officer present.

Gale again told the guy to get down on the ground. It was obvious he was going to try to run away. I then learned one of the most important lessons of my thirty-year career. This lesson probably saved my life on more than one occasion.

I saw Gale take one step back and then he kicked the suspect in his nuts as hard as he could, like he was punting a football. The sound of his foot kicking the suspect's groin sounded like someone kicking a bag of rice.

There was no mistake in knowing the kick found its target by the sound of the dull thud it made. The suspect fell to the ground like a deck of cards. He was then immediately handcuffed.

This was my first experience seeing what it takes to arrest a real bad guy. Once he was in handcuffs, I found a loaded handgun in the suspect's waistband. I then realized how close we came to getting shot that night.

Gale wrote in his crime report that he kicked the suspect in the groin, because he was possibly armed and not complying with orders to lie down. Nothing was ever said about those techniques in the old days.

In the future, if a gun was used in a crime, I made it a practice not to play around with the suspect. I always reacted fast to take the suspect down any way I could. This was because of the lesson I learned from Gale that night.

If a guy has a gun, either take him down or shoot his ass, don't waste time and try to talk to him. Gale wrote me a letter of commendation for helping him by calling a great pursuit and helping run down the armed suspect.

Remembering how fun it was that night still brings a smile to my face. I was a young cop being recognized for a good job on my first pursuit. Our old captain even listened to the pursuit on the radio and said "good job, kid" at the end of shift, which made me feel great.

The letter I received from Gale inspired me to write a variety of letters to other officers during my career. A small note of thanks will never be forgotten. A congratulation after a child is born, or a personal thought after a death in the family, will be treasured for life.

## Chapter 12
## Flat Tires

I loved to get into a good vehicle pursuit, like most young cops. It was not uncommon to have ten marked units chasing a car during a graveyard pursuit. Patrol sergeants almost never canceled pursuits. In the old days, they didn't care how many units were involved, as long as they didn't crash.

Some car chases looked like a Christmas tree speeding down the street, with so many patrol cars flashing their red and blue lights. These days, common practice is to have only three police cars maximum in most pursuits.

One car chase ended with the city paying for a lot of flat tires. During the pursuit, the suspect drove a stolen car through a drive-in-theater's exit, bending the ground spikes backwards.

The cops drove through the normal entrance. Eventually the suspect was stopped and arrested, after a chase up and down over the bumps. The show ended and the patrons and squad cars were leaving out the exit.

The ten cop cars drove out the exit, not knowing that all their tires were being popped by the security ground spikes. Numerous theater patrons who drove out the exit also got flat tires. Needless to say, the watch commander was pissed off at the dumb rookie officers who got flat tires.

## Chapter 13
## Bad Ending

Vehicle pursuits are one of the most hazardous things a cop can be involved in. The unpredictability of the suspect's actions makes any chase an extreme danger to the police and the public.

The change in national police pursuit tactics has made them safer over the years; however, sometimes they still end in death or serious injury. During pursuits, suspects do some really unpredictable things.

The tragic ending of one car chase, which occurred later in my career, left me with a permanent mental scar. The horrible memory of that incident is forever embedded in my mind, like a rock stuck in concrete.

One late night, I ran a stolen vehicle check on a large flatbed truck I was following on a rural road just inside the city limits. The vehicle information came back as stolen. The driver accelerated in an attempt to get away before I activated my overhead emergency lights and siren.

During the chase, the suspect drove the truck off a small two-lane bridge, causing it to roll over on its top. The driver crawled out the back window and ran into some bushes, while the female passenger was moaning in extreme pain from inside the truck.

I was alone and my main concern was for the passenger who was still in the truck. I ran toward the sound of the wailing passenger, only to find that she had been partially ejected and her torso was pinned under the truck.

Only the lower half of her body was visible, twisting around in pain. The top half of her body had to have been crushed under the truck's cab. I called for a heavy-duty hydraulic jack from the fire department to lift the large truck off the passenger.

Her moans were getting weaker and weaker. I bent over, leaned under the truck, and told her an ambulance was on the way. She probably couldn't understand me in her condition, but I wanted to give her some hope.

I had heard the same type of death gurgle before at other fatal car accidents and knew she was in bad shape. Her moans faded away, and she stopped moving. She died while I was telling her she would be okay.

Seeing someone die right in front of you takes your breath away. It's an ugly spectacle that makes you sick to your stomach. I felt guilty for initiating the pursuit that cost the passenger her life. Some experiences during my career didn't go away at the end of shift. In fact, many any of them have stayed with me long after retirement.

## Chapter 14
## Practical Jokes

Some of the practical jokes we played on each other during our rookie years would get us fired today. I seemed to be the butt of many jokes, most of which were centered on my patrol car. During the holiday season, I once found five Christmas trees wedged inside the rear seat.

One night while I was having Code -7, a friendly drunk was placed on the rear floorboard of my squad car and covered with a blanket. The culprits also replaced the patrol car's map lightbulb on the dashboard with a camera flashbulb.

When I drove away from Code -7, I heard the old guy moving around in the rear seat. I turned on the map light, only to be blinded for several seconds from the flashbulb going off next to my face. The drunk sat up and said, "God bless you, Mike." I always checked my back seat after my C-7 from then on. Cops have a juvenile sense of humor in many ways.

Putting several rocks inside all four hubcaps while a cop was away from his car was always good for a few laughs. The rocks make an enormous clanking and banging sound, which makes the driver think his car is falling apart.

Many cops have put paper confetti inside another cop's car defroster in the wintertime. It looks like a happy new year when the defroster is turned on, blowing paper all over the car. The joke is especially effective when your friend has a good looking ride-along that they're trying to impress.

During my younger years, I played more than my share of jokes on my patrol sergeants. One such joke almost got me a day off. I was sick and tired of our new lazy sergeant, who would spend half the shift at a coffee shop trying to pick up on the newest waitress. He was never around when you needed him.

I tied a dead duck onto the sergeant's car interior trunk latch. I tied the duck's wings wide open with a stick and a string. Another string was attached around the duck's neck and the trunk latch.

Our police car's trunks could be opened by pushing a button from inside of the car. Once the trunk opened, the duck would swing into view, hanging by his neck with wings spread open.

Little did I know that my sergeant's common practice was to back his patrol car up to the front window of a crowded Denny's restaurant and pop open his trunk to look for some paperwork.

It must have worked like a charm. A waitress later told me she heard loud gasps from several customers when they saw the spread-winged, dead duck swinging from the open trunk. The sergeant, of course, blamed me for the incident and chewed my ass out.

The graveyard watch commander was sixty-five years old and had over thirty-five years in the department. Rookie officers would not even say hi to him because he was so damn intimidating. He was a grouchy old bastard that liked to mess with the young cops. I didn't even like looking at him when we passed in the hallway.

The old fart used to take a nap in his unmarked vehicle in the same remote parking lot near the end of the shift. One night, I, along with several other young cops on my team, snuck up on the commander's car while he slept. We draped two large wool blankets over all the windows, making it pitch black inside.

After our shift was over, several of us got dressed and waited around for thirty minutes for the commander to drive into the station. We got worried when he didn't show up. The next day our sergeant told us the commander was over an hour late getting into the station, and was very pissed off.

We were then told the commander wanted to see us in his office. Up until this point, none of us had ever even talked to the commander.

We entered his office, and he snapped at us, "Shut my door and sit down." I felt like the Cowardly Lion in the Wizard of Oz, talking to the man behind the curtain.

We were about to shit our pants when the old commander started laughing. The commander told us he kept waking up from his nap in the car, only to find it was still dark out. He further said he woke up to a lady knocking on his blanket covered window, asking him if he was all right.

Luckily, the commander had a sense of humor and turned out to be a great guy. He would later share many of his own stories with us over a beer. The things the old cops got away with in the 1950s and 1960s made us feel like choir boys compared to them.

Years later, several hundred people attended his funeral. The story of the blanket was not told, but I knew a few of us still remembered it. It was a sad day because a lot of cops loved that grouchy old fart, even though he used to scare the hell out of us.

## Chapter 15
## McDonald's

McDonald's was a great friend to thousands of cops. All cops knew they could count on any McDonald's for free food. There was proper police etiquette. We did not go to the same restaurant more than once a week. We did this in order not to burn them out and take advantage of their generosity.

One cheap cop with over thirty years in the department went to the same McDonald's every morning as soon as he left roll call. That pissed all the other cops off. It looked bad having two or three patrol cars lined up at the drive-through at the same time.

A lot of the cops I worked with were Vietnam War Veterans. Most of them didn't take shit from anyone, and some were a little crazy. The constant eye blinking or twitching and the exaggerated startle reflex made it obvious which officers were affected by the war. They all shared a common bond and called each other brother. They were also the best cops in our department.

One such officer, David, took pride in showing his scrapbook of all the dead bodies he saw. Some of them he'd killed. It was easy to see he was reliving the stories by how pumped up he became. To say David was a little off would be a slight understatement, but he was a very good cop.

David decided to teach that old cop a lesson for going to McDonald's every single morning. He knew the morning manager well, because he was no stranger from eating there more than a few times himself.

David then played a great practical joke. This joke went down in our department's history as one of the all-time greats.

David hid his police car around the corner from the restaurant after roll call. He then explained to the manager his plan to have a little fun with the old cop. The manager was more than glad to help, as he was tired of feeding the old fart every day.

David stood behind the counter by the drive-through speaker and took the cop's order. The half-asleep old cop couldn't see David from his position in line with the other cars.

The old cop ordered his usual scrambled eggs, hash browns, sausage, and coffee. David told the older cop that McDonald's was out of eggs that morning, and he would have to order something else.

That pissed the old cop off. In a loud, rude voice, he then ordered pancakes, hash browns, sausage and coffee. David didn't miss a beat and responded with one of the best come backs ever. He advised the old cop that he had just told him they were out of eggs.

David then asked the old cop if eggs were in pancakes. More than a little annoyed, the old cop thought for a second and replied over the speaker, "Of course, eggs are in pancakes."

David then yelled through the speaker, "You stupid jerk, how can you have pancakes if we're out of eggs? Now order something else."

He couldn't believe his ears that some zit faced punk, who worked at McDonald's, had just told him off. The old cop then sped up to the drive-through window to yell at the worker, only to find David standing at the window, dressed in his uniform, laughing hysterically.

The old-timer then peeled out from the drive-through, never to be seen by that McDonald's staff again. He, of course, started going to another McDonald's down the street every morning. You can't change the stripes on a zebra.

## Chapter 16
## Family Fights

When I started on the job, the radio code for a family disturbance was a 415f call. Officers would contact all involved parties and use a technique called "Crisis and Intervention". Officers were taught to be counselors. They would separate each person and get their sides of the dispute. The cops would then have the couple come together to talk and find a solution or resolution to their problem.

Thousands of cops throughout the country learned crisis and intervention techniques. It only took a few years for the law enforcement community to figure out it didn't work. The basis of the technique is to rationalize with the people you're talking to, which looked good on paper.

It sounded like a good way to solve family fights if sober people were involved in the disturbance. In many 415f calls, one or both of the parties had been drinking. As any cop will tell you, trying to rationalize with a drunk is a waste of time.

The older officers went to the family fight calls, and within minutes gave one of the disputants a ride to a relative or friend's house to calm down and sober up. This was the standard procedure for family fight calls, even when the wife was slapped around a little. Cops knew it was futile to make an arrest because in most cases, the victim wouldn't follow up and prosecute.

The victim had to live and be supported by the guy who just slapped her around. Having three kids by him, no job, and nowhere to go, she didn't want him to go to jail. Plus, she knew when he got out of jail, he would beat the hell out of her again.

For years, most cops used this technique. Unfortunately, this procedure cost the lives of many young women nationwide. All too often, the chronic fights would go undocumented. The violence in family fights escalates with time and continues from one generation to the next.

It may start out with just harsh words during a fight. The next time the victim may get pushed to the ground, or a slapped in the face. All too often, the victim has later been beaten or even killed by their loving spouse.

Cops no longer have any discretion in what are now called domestic violence calls. If the couple is living together and meets the criterion, the officers must make a felony arrest for spousal abuse.

If there are any of the slightest signs of a visible injury, such as a red face or welt, the officer must make an arrest or be in big trouble. Even the threat of physical violence could get a person put in jail, depending on the circumstances. This regulation may seem harsh, but it has saved countless lives.

The violent, reoccurring beatings happen because people still get drunk and stupid. Nowadays, even the biggest asshole knows if he hits his old lady and the police are called, he's going to jail for a felony. Even if the victim does not want to press charges, which they often don't, the cops have no discretion over the mandatory arrest.

## Chapter 17
## First 187

I can still remember going on my first 187 homicide. It was on my first night out on my own. Most of my patrol team were from the same academy and were all very inexperienced.

The radio call came out as a husband-and-wife domestic dispute. A lady called in to report that her neighbors were having a loud argument next door. Two other young officers and I responded to the address.

We couldn't hear any arguments as we walked up to the residence, so we knocked on the front door. A few seconds later, a young man holding a baby answered the door. He handed the baby to one of the other officers and said, "My wife is in there."

I entered the living room to talk to the wife and get her side of the dispute. Certain things are set in a cop's brain for life, a permanent memory. The shock of seeing something unexpected is something you will never forget.

When I entered the living room, I found the man's wife lying on the couch. She had been shot ten times in the head with a rifle just a few seconds before we arrived.

I was stunned, as I did not expect to find a dead lady with half her face missing. I walked outside and handcuffed the docile husband, who confessed to killing his wife.

It didn't take me long to learn some people will kill another person over nothing of great importance. We learned the husband was upset at his wife for giving their neighbor five dollars for beer. The argument got violent because they were both drinking a lot. He shot her because he warned her not to give their money away again.

We learned an important lesson that day. The neighbor who phoned the dispute into the police later told the investigators she heard the gunshots just as the police cars turned on to her street.

We should have talked to the neighbor before we contacted the disputants. We were lucky that day, the husband only wanted to kill his wife. I could never understand how a man could kill his wife over five dollars.

Later on in life, I had many of my own heated arguments with my wife over money. I never hit my wife, but I understood how some people could lose their temper and do something they would regret for life.

## Chapter 18
## My First Shooting

One night, two other officers and I responded to a call about a man shooting a gun in front of his house. Being young, we drove up without lights on and parked around the block. We walked up to the address using available objects, such as trees and cars, as cover and concealment.

While we walked up to the house, a man in his 50s came out the front door. He was holding a pistol in his right hand. We all yelled at him to drop the gun. To our surprise, the man raised the gun, pointed it at the other two officers, and fired four shots at them.

All three of us returned fire with our six-shot 38 caliber revolvers. We knew we had to have hit the suspect because we were so close to him. We fired a total of eighteen rounds at the guy, who turned around, walked back inside his residence, and closed the door.

This was not like the movies. He didn't fly backwards against the wall from being shot, with blood flying everywhere. The man had been hit twice, but we didn't know it because of his non-reaction.

A tactical mistake I made could have got my friend killed. The suspect moved to a bedroom window and again started shooting at us. We returned fire while I was standing behind a tree and my friend was pinned down below the window the suspect was shooting out of.

I saw the suspect standing a few feet above my kneeling friend. I, with my infinite wisdom, yelled at him, "The suspect is right above you." Luckily, the suspect didn't hear my big mouth. He could have reached out the window and shot my friend in the head.

I then made another strategic mistake. I yelled at the officers to reload, because we each had fired six rounds. Letting the suspect know our guns were empty could have been a fatal mistake.

The guy was drunk and eventually exited his house and was arrested. The man shot at us six times from two different locations. Investigators determined one shot missed an officer's head by inches, after he showed them where he was standing during the shooting. They found a bullet hole in the wall next to where his head had been.

The other two officers and I went to the station and gave our statements to the detectives. When someone is injured as a result of an officer involved shooting, an investigator from the District Attorney Office will respond and listen to the interview along with a representative from the Police Officer Association.

The Detective gave me two admonishments. The first was that failure to answer any questions could be considered an act of misconduct and result in my termination. Reading me my "Miranda" rights was the second.

The Homicide Unit and Internal Affairs handled the detailed investigation that night. I was nervous about the investigation even though I didn't do anything wrong.

It was four in the morning when I left the department to go home. I thought of stopping off at an all-night market to get a beer, but it was after the legal time to sell alcohol.

The next day, my landlord came over to visit. He was a World War II combat veteran who saw more than his share of action. Filled with excitement, I told the old guy about my shooting the night before.

I was still pumped up on the adrenalin high. The old guy gave me some of the best advice that I ever received in my career. He realized the shooting was the biggest thing I had been involved in as a young officer.

The old timer told me I wasn't the first or last cop to get into a shooting. It wasn't that big of a thing. My bubble began to burst. He explained that our country has had thousands of brave soldiers face bombs and machine gun fire while running into danger throughout our many wars. My incident was tame compared to a wartime firefight.

The landlord told me that a lot of people have been in shootings, and things could have been much worse. It still took me several days to come down from the excitement of the call.

I soon craved the high I got from hot calls. My need for excitement was just as addictive as heroin was to an addict. Going to the most dangerous calls I could was a regular occurrence.

The scarier the call or pursuit, the better the adrenalin high was. Pretty soon stolen car stops were boring, and they didn't even get my pulse rate up. Business robberies and shootings were my favorite calls to go on. Any gun call in the city was a priority for me to go to.

Several weeks later, I talked with one of the other young officers who was in the shooting with me. He told me that the day after the shooting, he thought about quitting the department. The shooting left him feeling scared, and he thought he wasn't cut out to be a cop.

That officer did not quit and went on to become one of the best captains in our department. Most officers didn't know that fear is a very common stress reaction after a shooting. According to statistics, if a person dies from a shooting, a lot of cops retire.

Little was known about how to care for a cop after a critical incident in those days. That rookie officer was involved in four more shootings before being promoted to sergeant.

My old-time lieutenant told me it was mandatory for any officer who gets into a shooting to see a shrink. The lieutenant then said, "Psychobabble was a bunch of bullshit," and for me to tell the doctor I was fine, so I could get back to work. I told the doctor I was okay and was back at work the next day. Officers did not get any time off after a shooting, unless the suspect was killed.

The man had no criminal record. We got our first taste of plea bargaining when we went to court. This would be the first of many times the District Attorney's Office would piss us off. Accepting pathetic plea offers and dropping cases would soon become the norm.

The man pled guilty for two counts of attempted murder of three police officers. The district attorney accepted a one-year sentence. After several years, I learned not to get upset over any case. The attorneys had stacks of cases on their desks, and were trying to do the best they could. It does not matter if a suspect goes free or not, because there will be many other crooks to take their place.

## Chapter 19
## Stress Reactions

After my shooting, I was driving home when something weird happened to me. I was just starting to relax and replay the shooting in my mind when my right hand began shaking. The shaking lasted for about ten minutes. I got scared because I couldn't stop it and thought I was having a medical problem. I didn't know I was having a common stress reaction, which some people experience after a critical incident.

Much later I learned that stress reactions can appear immediately after a traumatic event, or in other cases may appear days, weeks and sometimes even years later. The duration of stress reactions may be short or long-term depending on the severity of the event and an individual's coping abilities.

Signs of stress are individualistic, and vary from one person to another. Some people under stress may exhibit little, if any, signs except to someone trained in stress recognition.

## Chapter 20,
## The Sad Call

After being on the force a few years, I had
already gone on numerous calls where I saw
dead bodies. The people died from a variety of
causes and under different circumstances. Car
crashes, industrial accidents, homicides,
suicides, and old age were some of the more
common reasons.

Some suicides were horrible to look at.
One guy sat on some train tracks facing an
oncoming train. The other officers and I only
found small pieces of his body scattered down
the tracks for several hundred yards.

Another old guy placed a 12-gauge
shotgun under his chin and blew the top of his
head off. His brains were embedded in the
living room ceiling and dripping down while I
was looking into an empty skull.

Jumpers were always messy to look at
after they hit the pavement. A young couple
once jumped together out of a twenty-story
hotel window. When I got there, it was hard to
tell which body part belonged to which person.

The dead bodies never bothered me very
much. I always felt a deep compassion for the
friends and family who had to deal with the

pain of losing a loved one. I could feel their pain, as it reminded me of the vivid memories of my father's unexpected death.

One New Year's Eve, I signed up to work overtime. My wife didn't mind me working a lot because she liked the extra money. This would be the worst night of my career. This was the only night where I cried after I finished a call.

I got a radio call a little after midnight. The dispatcher gave the code "926" for a dead body from an apparent suicide. As most experienced cops know, it's not uncommon to have suicides during the holiday season. People who live alone reflect on better times and then they kill themselves for many reasons.

I drove up to the residence a few minutes after the fire and ambulance arrived. I walked through the front door, and was surprised to see the paramedics doing CPR on a seventeen-year-old boy.

The kid's face was blue due to lack of oxygen, and it was obvious he was already dead. I knew the standard procedure was for the paramedics to continue CPR until they got to the emergency room.

The kid's mother and fourteen-year-old brother were in a bedroom, out of sight of the living room. The ambulance crew transported the juvenile to the hospital. I was sure glad I was almost finished with this call. I just needed to get some names and other information from the mother, which would not take long.

Once I entered the bedroom, I met both the mother and her other son, Jason. The younger boy asked me if Jimmy was going to be all right. Neither of them had any idea Jimmy passed away. I told them I didn't know how Jimmy was doing, but the hospital staff could advise them on his condition.

I collected the necessary information for the report from the mother. She told me that Jimmy had a fight with his girlfriend and was in his room for most of the night.

At midnight she went inside her son's bedroom to wish him a happy New Year. The mother said at first she couldn't see her son. She then opened a closet door and found him hanging, with a belt tied around his neck.

The mother said she and Jason pulled him down and called the ambulance. Jason was crying next to his mom and kept repeating, "It was my fault." I later found out the two brothers had argued just before Jimmy went into his bedroom.

I stood up to leave and asked the mother if there was anything else I could do for her. Thinking she would say no and drive herself to the hospital, I was, again, grateful this call was almost over.

The mother then asked me for a ride to the hospital because she had no car. She also asked if they could drop Jason off at one of his friend's house a few blocks away.

I couldn't say no to the mother. I then dropped Jason off and gave her a ride to the hospital. We didn't talk much during the ride. I didn't know what to say. Once at the hospital, I contacted the doctor in charge and was told the kid was dead on arrival.

The doctor then told me he had several critically injured people being transported to the hospital from a major car accident. Since it was New Year's Eve, the place was already packed with hurt people in the hallways.

He asked me to tell the mother her son died because he didn't have the time to talk to her. Then the doctor walked down the hall to treat the other patients. I had never given a death notification to anyone before. I sure as hell didn't want to in this case. How do you tell a mother her son has died?

The mother was waiting in a small room by herself when I entered. Without saying a word, it only took her a few seconds to look at my face and know her oldest son was dead.

The mother started crying, as did I. We hugged each without saying a word. We both just needed the comfort of a human's touch. We didn't talk a lot as I drove her home.

I had experienced the mental trauma and emotional shock she was in when my dad died.

I knew sometimes a person does not feel like talking.

The mother then stunned me with her next request. She told me that Jason idolized his older brother. The mother said she could not tell him his brother had died.

She asked me to tell Jason that his brother had passed away. I was never taught in the academy how to handle such a call, but my heart told me I had to.

I dropped the mother off at her house and drove over to pick Jason up. Jason was already waiting in the front yard. He ran up to the passenger side window of my patrol car and frantically asked if Jimmy was going to be all right. The poor kid didn't have a clue his brother was dead.

I asked Jason to sit in the car while we drove around for the next thirty minutes. I told Jason how my dad died in my arms and how sometimes life doesn't seem fair. Jason looked at me with tears running down his face. He then asked if his brother had died.

I explained that his body had passed away, but his soul would live on for eternity. I assured him that they would see each other again when the time was right. For the second time in one night, I found myself crying and hugging a stranger.

After I dropped Jason off at his home, I drove around the corner and parked my squad car in an alley. I again started crying. I thought no job could pay me enough to go through that type of experience a second time.

Then it was off to the next call.

## Chapter 21
## 211 In Progress

My first FTO told me to never let my guard down during my shift. Cops have been killed driving to and from work, while wearing their uniforms. Other times, officers have engaged in shootings in their own police department lobbies and parking lots.

Being shot while eating or having their Code-7 is something that has happened to more than one on-duty cop. Police officers never know when some nut will try to shoot them.

Most cops love free donuts and hot coffee. I had a bad habit of walking into businesses without looking around first. One late night, I parked at the rear of a donut shop to be out of any supervisor's view who may have driven by.

I walked up to the front door and saw a large man standing at the counter. The guy would look around, then point at a donut. Call it a gut feeling or just dumb luck. I stood outside the door and watched him for a few seconds.

He would periodically look out the window and stare up and down the street. I watched him point at another donut and again look up and down the street, while holding his right hand in his coat pocket.

Realizing the crook was about to rob the business and was holding a gun in his coat, I reached for my portable radio to ask for help. The suspect then looked over his shoulder and saw me standing by the door.

The guy was most likely on parole, because he was as big as a brick shit house. I was in a really bad spot. My dispatcher had no idea where I was. He started walking towards the door, still holding his hand in his coat pocket.

I played it cool and held the door open for him. He said, "Thank you," and took one step outside. Once he walked past me, I placed my revolver against the back of his head. I told him to get on the ground or I would have to shoot him. He went down on the pavement without saying a word.

I then reached into his coat to remove the gun that I thought he was holding. To my great surprise, I only found a set of car keys in his coat. As I continued to search the suspect, he didn't say a word.

I knew I would get some days off for sticking my gun to an innocent fellow's head. There was nothing I could arrest him for. My big mistake was following up on my stupid gut instincts. How could I screw up so royally, I wondered?

As I was patting him down for weapons, I felt a small bulge below the dude's waist band area. My gun was still on the back of his head, but I still had not called for help. I asked the guy if he was on parole and if he had a gun in his pants.

He told me he was on parole for armed robbery and had a gun in his pants. I then handcuffed the suspect, who was very cooperative. I arrested him for attempted robbery and later took his statement at the department.

The middle-aged man had been arrested many times, and had served a combined total of fifteen years in prison. He had just got out of the joint the prior week and said if he was convicted of this new crime, he would go to prison for life under the career criminal law.

The suspect was calm and showed no anger or animosity towards me. I gave him a soda, a cigarette, and a little respect during the interview. I thanked him for being polite and we began to talk.

At the end of our contact with each other, the parolee thanked me for treating him fairly during the arrest. I had several close relatives who had been to prison, and I knew they weren't bad people. I had also been trained to never trust any parolee. You can give a parolee respect, but never turn your back on them.

The man then told me something that I never forgot. Maybe it was just macho prison talk, or maybe he was trying to give me some good advice. He told me if I had walked into that donut shop while it was being robbed, he would have shot me in the head as fast as he could. I knew he was dead serious.

The old-time crook told me he often planned his next robbery while in prison, and thought about tactics and how he would react if confronted with the police. Convicts have a lot of time to think about how to commit their next crime while doing time in the joint.

Knowing he would go back to prison for life, he had nothing to lose by shooting a cop. Plus, it would give him special status in prison. He said, "It was nothing personal, it was just business."

For the rest of my career, I always paused before walking into any business.

## Chapter 22
## Very Tempting Call

A lot of my married friends had a girl they saw on the side. Some cops made it a practice to try to pick up every good looking waitress at restaurants that gave us a good deal. I was always shy and ugly, which prevented me from trying to pick up on even a blind lady. I also was old fashioned and thought cheating on my wife was wrong.

One night I was dispatched to a peeping tom call. I arrived at the apartment complex and knocked on the door in order to take a short report, which would only take a few minutes. Apparently, someone had been looking in the complainant's front window at night.

Once the door opened, a beautiful girl around nineteen greeted me. She had long dark hair and the face of an angel. This poor girl was only wearing a short tank top, with no bra, and a pair of white shorts that barely covered her ass.

She asked me inside her apartment. She then asked me to sit down, pointing to a small living room chair. I was more than a bit surprised when she sat down on the floor in front of me. She crossed her legs, Indian style, which made her pants even tighter. It was impossible to look down at her and not see her breasts as she talked. I tried not to look, but I was losing an uphill battle that I didn't want to win.

This cute little thing then told me about a guy who had been looking at her through her living room window for the last several weeks. She then unfolded a handwritten note that the suspect left for her.

She said she would read me the note if I wanted her to. I had no idea what it said and told her to read it. It read "I have been watching you sitting at your kitchen table only wearing your panties and no bra. I have seen you touch your pussy and tits at times. I love your long hair and dream about wrapping it around my cock."

The complainant's head was only a few feet from my groin while she read this sensuous note. She then shook her hair from side to side and said, "He must have seen me do this a lot." She started to read the note again.

It got really graphic, at which time I had to stop her. It's not that I didn't want to hear the rest of it; however, I had such a hard on that I was in fear of her seeing my pants sticking up like a tent pole.

I asked her for the note, so I could book it into evidence. A fear then came over me on how I was going to stand up without her seeing my full-blown erection. I made small talk in order to kill time. This girl was still sitting in front of me like she wanted to give me a blow job.

Covering my groin with my clipboard I walked to the door, half bent over. I looked at my watch and saw I'd been in her apartment for forty-five minutes. *What a waste of time*, I thought. Maybe I should have taken a chance and had sex with her?

I remember one older cop tell me, "Your badge can get you pussy, but pussy can get your badge." Another friend of mine, who cheated on his wife once, told me he felt so ashamed and dirty that he couldn't look her in the eyes.

He gave me good advice and told me to never cheat on my wife because it wasn't worth the bad feelings. In my twenty-nine-year marriage, I never kissed any other woman, however, I wanted to several times.

## Chapter 23
## Peeping Tom

When I worked downtown one year, we had a rash of "Peeping Tom" calls in one neighborhood.

The suspect description was always the same: a male white in his twenties, with long blonde hair. The suspect would look through single women's bedroom windows and masturbate on their walls. All the calls were around three in the morning.

A friend out of my academy, Dean, and I spent several weeks trying to find this pervert. One night, at three in the morning, we got our break. A radio call matching the suspect's description came in close to where we were both parked. The suspect was prowling around in the rear of a single girl's home.

We drove up quietly because you can hear a car's engine from blocks away on graveyard. We turned off our lights and parked a half-a-block down the street. As we walked down the alley, we talked about who would give the radio transmissions if it turned into a foot pursuit.

We didn't make a sound while sneaking up on the guy, who was still looking through a window at a pretty college-aged girl. The suspect turned around and found us both standing right behind him in the dark shadows.

There is no statute of limitations for civil rights violations for excessive force. I will only say the suspect struggled during the arrest. We only used the minimal amount of force necessary to make the arrest. The nurse at the jail did what she could for his abrasions.

The suspect's arrest record was insane. He had numerous burglary, auto theft, and prowling convictions. This young man had already served two years in a youth prison and was only nineteen years old. He was convicted on our call since he was on probation for prowling and received six months in jail.

It must have been six months to the day when we got another call of a "Peeping Tom" at three in the morning, in the same target area. The description was of a male white with short hair. The suspect had to get a haircut while in jail.

My same friend Dean and I used the same tactics as last time. We snuck up on the poor guy, like a cat preying on a bird. He didn't have a chance when we jumped on his ass and began using a lot of minimal force. The only thing the suspect said was "Shit, not you two again."

Minimal force must hurt because his screams attracted the attention of a man and woman who were sitting on their rear porch a few feet behind us. They were watching us take the suspect into custody, much to our surprise.

The couple was in their eighties and asked if everything was okay. We were a little concerned about our minimal force witnesses. We told them the suspect was arrested for masturbating while looking at their female neighbor through her bedroom window. The couple was shocked and thanked us for doing such a good job. Either they were blind or great supporters of the police.

## Chapter 24
## Why the Kids

Every cop's worst call is where they see a dead child. Each summer, many cops have to see some poor little kid's lifeless body being pulled out of a swimming pool. It hits home when the cop has a child of their own who may be the same sex or age as the drowning victim they just did CPR on. A sad part of being a cop is when they learn, "Life isn't always fair to innocent children."

Identification with the victims or their family is often a big problem in police work. Some cops do a better job at handling the stress of the job than other cops. Each individual cop handles the death of a child or any other horrible call in their own way. Just because a person doesn't cry, doesn't mean they're not grieving.

Cops see so many deaths and injuries, they understand accidents happen from time to time. Some cops seek comfort and call it God's will to take children. Others just realize accidents are a part of life.

What pisses cops off the most is the innocent taking of a child's life. Most cops have seen the horrible results of a stressed-out parent who kills their entire family. Cops always think, "Why did he have to kill the kids?"

My first encounter with a homicide and suicide call is one which I will always remember. A well-to-do business owner had separated from his wife several weeks earlier.

He had never been arrested before and was a respected community leader. The couple had two children, a seven-year-old boy and five-year-old girl.

One late night, the man left his children asleep in their beds and drove to his wife's new apartment. Once he arrived, he kicked open the apartment door and ran into her bedroom.

The husband shot his wife in the face and then shot her new boyfriend several times with a 357 magnum, killing them both. A witness saw the suspect vehicle leaving, called the police, and gave them the license number.

Several officers and I responded to the registered owner's address of the suspect vehicle. We arrived at the nice home, which was in an upscale neighborhood, and found the car in the driveway.

I took a position in the rear yard while other officers established a perimeter around the large house. We were going to wait for the SWAT team, which had already been called out.

For some rookie reason, I took a position where I could look into the living room through a large sliding glass window. I was stunned for a second at what I saw.

The father and both of his children were lying face down on the living room floor. One child was on each side of the father, who had one arm resting over each child's back. They were all lying next to each other.

Each child and the father were shot one time in the head. I entered the living room to check for any pulse even though it was obvious, because of the head trauma and scattered brain tissue, that they were all dead.

The suspect had returned home after killing his wife. He then shot his kids and himself in the living room. The neighbors, who were later interviewed, said they heard three shots just before the police arrived.

To everyone's surprise, the paramedics found the suspect still had a pulse. The patrol sergeant told me to ride in the ambulance with the suspect and collect his clothes at the hospital. The suspect shot himself in his right temple.

Once at the hospital, an X-ray showed the bullet traveled through the guy's brain, but he was still alive. The doctor in charge told me that there was no chance the suspect would survive. He could die at any time.

The doctor then told the nurse to give the suspect a shot of morphine on the remote chance he could still feel pain. The older nurse drew back the curtains, so only she and I were in the room.

She drew up the morphine in the syringe as directed while I gathered the guy's clothes for evidence. The nurse then did something that I always admired.

She asked me if it was true this guy had just killed his two small children. I told her he shot them both in their heads. She then pointed the syringe upwards and squirted the morphine across the room. She said, "He would be fine now."

I loved that nurse for doing that. I had to live with seeing those two small kids in my mind for the rest of my life, but I could always smile, remembering what the nurse did.

## Chapter 25
## Smart Crook

One Halloween night, our sector had eight armed robberies within several hours. One suspect, who robbed a gas station, dressed up like a vampire. Witnesses followed the vampire suspect on foot, straight from the gas station to an apartment.

The police were called, and the witnesses identified the man, still dressed as a vampire. We then searched the small one-bedroom apartment for an hour for the 25 caliber semi-automatic handgun he used and the cash taken from the register.

The money and gun had to be inside the apartment, but we couldn't find anything. The suspect, who was on parole, was arrested and booked in the county jail. A few weeks later, I went to the preliminary hearing and talked with a deputy district attorney in his office before court started.

I learned the suspect's girlfriend was later arrested for narcotics. She made a deal with the district attorney for a lighter sentence if she helped them in the Halloween robbery case.

The girlfriend said she was in the apartment when the suspect hid the gun and money. She said once the suspect knew the police were outside the apartment; he opened the refrigerator and removed a fresh head of lettuce. The suspect hollowed out a plug in the middle of the head of lettuce and inserted the small gun and money inside the middle of it. He then reinserted the plug he carved out and placed the whole head in a large salad bowl. The guy even poured liquid salad dressing over the head of lettuce so the police would not touch it, which we didn't.

## Chapter 26
## Jessie

One night, about three in the morning, I was driving in a bad part of the city called Oak Park. The only people out that late were the newspaper delivery truck driver and crooks.

I was half asleep and looking for someone to talk to. If the truth were known, I would rather talk to the street people than most of the cops I worked around. The prostitutes and drunks could tell some very funny stories that were beyond imagination.

The cops were good people, but some had egos that made me sick. They thought they were better than everyone else and tried to prove it at every opportunity. It pissed me off when they treated some poor drunk rough or talked down to them.

This was a residential area with small stores on most corners. Boarded-up houses and abandoned cars were scattered throughout this part of town. Used condoms and broken beer bottles were lying in the tall weeds in the vacant lots.

On Friday nights, there would be a crowd of drunks, drug dealers, and prostitutes outside every store. Every crime a person could think of happened in that tiny little area. During the daytime, it looked like any other low-income neighborhood, with kids playing and people doing yard work. During the night, the two-legged animals would come out.

The good people had to stay in their homes for their own protection. Boarded-up houses became crack dens, with people getting high inside. Every single night was filled with the sound of gunshots, loud voices, and squealing car tires.

The drug houses stuck out like a fart in church. Several gang members, wearing their red clothes, would sit on the porch of some run-down house at all hours of the day and night. People in cars, riding bicycles, or walking on foot would visit for a few minutes. Then they'd be gone in a flash, with a small chunk of the white stuff called "rock cocaine."

The hard-core crackheads would hide their rock cocaine in their mouths or in their ass cracks in case the police stopped them after they bought some dope.

The variety of customers that we stopped after they bought drugs was amazing. I stopped teachers, lawyers, blue and white-collar workers of every type. On a few occasions, I even stopped a cop from another agency leaving a drug house.

This night had a cold chill in the air. Most of the street people were already wrapped up in their blankets, sleeping in some alley or doorway.

Over the years, I discovered drunks could find the strangest places to sleep. They'd find every nook and cranny between two buildings. They would look like a squirrel, sleeping in a little nest, made of cardboard scraps and rags for a blanket.

Then I saw a black guy walking down the sidewalk. He wasn't staggering or acting suspicious, but I had to talk to someone to keep from wrecking another squad car because I fell asleep again. I was running out of fake stories to use. I had already used a phony story of a dog running out in front of my car. Everyone knew I fell asleep, but the sergeant couldn't prove it. I didn't like to lie. I knew I couldn't tell the truth about falling asleep and wrecking a police cruiser. If that happened, it would mean days off, which I couldn't afford.

I drove behind the guy as he was walking along. My plan was to pull alongside of him and ask if he would mind talking to me for a few minutes. I'd have my gun out and hidden under my clipboard where he couldn't see it.

I was too damn lazy to get out of the car while talking to him. This was horrible officer safety and could have gotten me hurt or killed.

Some bad guy with a warrant or just some nut who hated cops could rush me sitting in my car.

In some ways, talking to people from inside the car put the people I was contacting at ease. They knew if I didn't get out of my car, I wasn't going to search them for drugs. Many street people had drugs in their possession.

If I got out of the car, some would run. Others would try to play it cool. They'd be calm until I started to conduct a pat down search, then they would run or fight.

That's why I had a habit of telling people I was not going to pat them down, because I didn't want to find anything illegal. I used this line of "bullshit" often to keep them from running. I would tell them it was time for me to go home.

Acting like a typical lazy cop, I'd say I didn't want to write a report and do overtime. I would tell them I just wanted to talk to them for a few minutes, and ask them to sit down and keep their hands in view. Most of the time, they would do what I asked. Other times they had the eyes of a scared rabbit and were just as fast.

I learned people would often run once I started to pat them down if they were holding something illegal. Patting people down for guns or dope when I was alone was something I didn't like to do.

Once I had to fight a guy over a gun I found in his pocket during a pat down. I was alone, and we were both rolling on the ground as we fought for the gun. I ended up head butting him in the face to make him let go. The crazy asshole was trying to kill me.

This old black guy I stopped looked like he was in his forties. He didn't have that typical muscular build, which many people fresh out of prison have. Maybe he wouldn't mind talking to some sleepy "peckerwood" cop.

I pulled alongside of him and asked if he had a few minutes to talk. He looked down at me as he continued to walk down the sidewalk. There was an annoyed look on his face.

The guy then asked me, "Why are you hassling me?" He didn't seem mad, but it was the sad tone in his voice that got me curious about what was wrong with him.

I gave him my standard line of bullshit about being a lazy cop that just wanted to talk. I told him I wouldn't pat him down and wasn't trying to mess with him. The guy stopped and sat down on the sidewalk. He crossed his feet and put his hand on top of his head. He didn't say a thing, but he looked like he had been through this many times before. Most black men have.

Then I saw a tear rolling down his cheek. He told me to run my warrant checks or do whatever I had to do, so he could go. I really felt bad for inconveniencing the guy.

Wanting him to understand I didn't mean to harass him in any way was important to me. I was sleepy and wanted to talk to someone to keep awake and kill some time before my shift was over.

The guy looked tired, as if he lived a rough life. He had more than his share of wrinkles on his face, much like me. As the poor soul looked up at me, he said he didn't mind talking to me as long as I didn't disrespect him.

It was all adding up now. The way he sat down and crossed his ankles and asked not to be disrespected were signs he had been to the joint. I stayed in my car while I talked to him for the first few minutes, to put him at ease.

My gun was still pointing at him, plus I could see his hands. He didn't appear to be a big threat to me. After a while, I got out of my squad car and sat on the front push bar while we talked.

I was correct. The old convict said he was just released from prison two weeks ago. He said he did ten years for an armed robbery and murder. After robbing a convenience store, his friend ran from a car with a gun and was shot and killed by the police.

He was charged with homicide because his accomplice was killed during the commission of a felony in which he took part. The man continued to tell me about his long criminal history.

My new friend's name was Jessie. He was named after Jesse Owens, the Olympic track star. Jessie had a chance of getting a college football scholarship, but his drug use prevented that dream. He grew up in a very rundown neighborhood in Oakland, with his kid brother Leon.

His little brother was one of the biggest "crack dealers" in town. He stood 6' 8" and weighed 260 pounds. Just like Jessie, he had been to prison several times. He also belonged to a gang called the Bloods. It was a dangerous life on the streets.

After going to the joint he joined the Black Guerilla Family prison gang for survival. Being small in size, he needed to be part of a gang for protection. Now he had to sell drugs and do other things for his gang.

This went on for years until he realized he was being played. He finally matured and saw the gang as a bunch of street thugs that had no future. He was tired of being a pawn.

The gang asked him to do a hit on a white guy who was an "Enforcer" in the Aryan Brotherhood prison gang. An enforcer is a gang's muscle man, a very mean and dangerous person. The gang uses these people to hurt other convicts who don't pay their debts or break prison rules.

The old guy sitting down near me spoke softly. He looked over his shoulder from time to time as he talked. He explained that he refused to do the hit for his gang. They put a contract out on him for not following orders.

He told the prison officials he was "dropping out" of his gang, which meant he would have to go through debriefing. This is when the drop-out tells all they know about their gang.

The drop-out is given a "snitch jacket" to everyone in prison and becomes a marked man. They become what is called a "hermit." This means every gang member has a duty to kill any drop-out on sight. This continues for life, in or out of prison, no questions asked. If a gang member doesn't kill him, they may be killed.

He told me he was sent to protective custody for the rest of his sentence. He was there only two weeks when another inmate tried to stab him with a small shank.

Another gang member, one he knew from his old gang, was ordered to kill him.

This meek little guy sitting down next to me said he grabbed the guy around his head while he was being stabbed. My new friend said he got stuck in the neck ten times by the prison-made knife. It was lucky for him the shank was made from a small plastic toothbrush that was melted down to have a sharp point.

The old guy then said something that sent my blood cold. As the big ass dude was stabbing him, he reached around and stuck his index finger in one of the guy's eye sockets. Popping the guy's eye out saved his life and ended the attack.

After being released from the hospital, the Prison Gang Unit questioned him about the attack. He refused to say anything at all. Being a bigger rat in prison would only make things worse for him.

Because of his refusal to cooperate and the severity of the injury, he was placed in the Security Housing Unit, or the SHU. This meant a tiny little one-person cell with no windows. Inmates spent twenty-three hours a day inside their cells, with very little to do.

They ate all their meals in their cells. Showering was even a luxury. They got out one hour a day to spend time in a tiny cage outside. They had no contact with other inmates. The guards didn't say much to the convicts either. There was just no one to talk with.

Having no socialization could drive a person insane. Jessie told me he did, in fact, go crazy after a month in the SHU. He found himself playing with his own feces one day. Jessie said he was holding a conversation with little piles of poop, while pretending they were people, when he realized he was stark raving mad.

Jessie was not happy and didn't want to live. The old guy was constantly trying to get up the nerve to hang himself. Anything was better than living in that small cell, even death.

In a brief moment of mental clarity, he looked down at what he was doing. Seeing his bizarre antics, he became repulsed at his own behavior and started to cry. He realized that he was in bad shape and had to do something. If he didn't find a way to occupy his mind, he would someday not be able to return to the real world.

* * *

Over the next few weeks, I met Leon several times in dark alleys while having long talks with Jessie. Leon may have been a drug dealer, but he respected me because I was fair to the street people. I knew he was into all kinds of illegal things and none of his friends liked the cops. A lot of street people hated any cop who wore a uniform, regardless if they knew them or not.

They only had bad experiences with the police their entire lives. Most street people grew up not to trust or like the police. Leon never disrespected or condemned me for wearing a badge. He always treated me like a friend and not a cop.

He was a top gang leader, which gave him the freedom to not give a shit what the others in his gang thought about him. If people had a problem with him, his crew could handle things. He had more than one crackhead that would kill on his order at the drop of a dime.

One day, Leon thanked me for being Jessie's friend. He explained that Jessie enjoyed talking to me about different things he experienced in life. Since Jessie got out of the joint, he'd become a loner and didn't talk to people in their neighborhood. Jessie didn't like many people, and trusted fewer. He had no real friends.

Leon said he noticed a big change in Jessie. Leon knew Jessie lost his mind in that tiny little room in the SHU. He knew his brother had been kept isolated from other prisoners, and even guards and other staff.

The SHU was the worst place to do time in prison. Even hard-core convicts were nervous about being sent there. Many of his friends told him how horrible the loneliness was in isolation. With no one to talk to, they would make up imaginary friends and hold regular conversations with them.

Leon then said something very strange, coming from a crack dealer to a cop. He told me if I ever needed some street help for anything, he would take care of me. I thanked him, knowing he was just trying to be nice to me.

I was thinking about how funny it was. The thought of asking a hardcore gang member for help with anything was amusing, to say the least. Later, I found myself in desperate need of his help.

\* \* \*

Over the next month, I had the chance to talk with Jessie many times in between my radio calls. It got to the point where I was looking forward to our talks. On my days off, I found myself thinking about what Jessie had told me.

The things he told me over the next several weeks enlightened me in ways I didn't think were possible. Certainly, an old crackhead on parole couldn't teach me these wonders of life. Or could he?

I longed to find the ability to obtain true happiness from my own mind, and not from a twelve-ounce bottle of beer. I needed his insight on happiness in order to gain my eternal peace.

Some days I would race off to find Jessie after rollcall was over. It scared me when I couldn't find him. I knew he was back on the crack pipe. Each time I saw him, he was a little dirtier and had that faraway look in his eye.

It would only be a matter of time before he was arrested again. I tried several times to get my friend to go to a drug rehabilitation center, but he knew he could never control his addiction. I'd try to find him between my radio calls. He'd turn up walking the streets or in some alley, and we would have our talk until I got a call.

During our talks, Jessie told me that in his small cell in prison, all of his senses were deprived of any pleasure. Nothing smelled good. The food tasted like shit. Nothing was pretty to look at, certainly not the guards. He got bored with listening to the music on a few compact disks he had. Even masturbation got old, plus it didn't take up much of his time.

He told me that while he was still in prison, he was half asleep when he thought of a funny childhood experience with his brother. He laughed out loud at the recollection of the hysterical event.

At that point, a thought passed through his mind and transformed his life, as well as mine, as I soon found out. Jessie said our mind controls our ability to have happiness. He said with long hours of practice, he learned to attain an internal happiness.

He learned to control his mind and experience any pleasure he wanted. Jesse could experience anything which his five senses enjoyed through his mind. It was as if the sensations he felt were happening in real life.

The smell of a flower, the taste of an orange, the sound of the ocean, the sight of a sunrise and the feel of a kiss, are the simple things that made my friend happy.

He later learned this ability was called astral projection. Jessie said our mind is our obvious sixth sense. I thought about it and knew he was correct. He then told me of things I thought were not possible for a human to do.

I knew he was telling the truth, because what he told me made so much sense. It was so simple to understand. I was not sure why I didn't discover the nature of his words earlier. They all were humble and true.

Jesse had to learn to survive in his mind if he wanted his body to live in prison. He then told me the secret of obtaining everlasting happiness from within and explained that most people are hostages to their egos.

Unfortunately, being a hostage to crack cocaine for most of his adult life, Jessie's main daily thought was about how he was going to get money to buy some dope. Sure, he still liked going to the movies or riding his bicycle, but nothing was fun unless he was high.

Jessie said most people are a hostage to one kind of pleasure or another. It may be food, sex, alcohol, or their job. A person must have balance in life. Too much of any single pleasure can be harmful.

Jessie then told me how he reached his inner happiness in order to survive in prison. He had to rely on his mind to find happiness. Jessie began meditating and going into a trance-like state of mind. He wasn't asleep because he was aware of the pleasure he was having, unlike any dream he ever had.

Jessie could actually taste food, feel the warmth of the sun, and experience any sensation he wished when he was in that state of mind. Jessie said he could fulfill any fantasy his mind could think of. He might fly over the highest mountain tops. He could make love to the most beautiful women imaginable.

Jessie told me the things he learned to do were all by using his sixth sense or his mind. The things he experienced were fun to do, however, they didn't bring him any closer to reaching inner peace. He desperately wanted

to graduate to the next plateau on his
journey for paradise.

Jessie went deep inside himself, and
thought of the pain and suffering he
caused others to have. He had brought so
much pain to people in his life. He cried at
wasting his life. It made him sick to his
stomach to think about all the drugs he
used. He did so many things that hurt so
many other people.

He could have made something of
himself. Jessie dreamed of becoming a
football player or a teacher. Maybe he
could somehow help other people.
Growing up, Jessie always liked helping
others in any way he could.

A thought then raced into Jessie's
mind. He remembered the funny thought
he had that made him laugh out loud in
isolation. That was what brought him back
to reality after he went insane in the SHU.

The thought was of how he once
surprised his younger brother at Christmas
time. He bought Leon a brand-new bicycle,
which was the best present he ever got in
his life.

Jessie mowed the neighbor's lawns
and did odd jobs for two months in order to
earn enough money to buy the bike. He
never forgot the happiness he felt for doing
something nice for his brother. In the

ghetto, life is rough for kids. People are sick with every kind of substance abuse imaginable.

Their mom was an alcoholic, and they never knew their dad. Christmas at their house wasn't much fun, as they never got very many presents, let alone a tree. Macaroni and cheese was their usual Christmas dinner.

He said he was like a father to Leon. He always looked out for him in their tough neighborhood. Jessie got into more than one fight protecting his little brother. This was something that Leon would never forget. He would do anything for Jessie, as I would later find out.

Jessie thought of the surprised look on his brother's face when he woke up and saw that shiny bicycle. That was one thing that truly made him happy in life.

He thought about that warm, intoxicating feeling he got out of bringing happiness to his brother. He realized, in a moment of mental clarity, the way to reach the next plateau in his quest to reach the ultimate inner peace.

It was so simple; he was mad at not realizing it before. He knew it would be extremely hard to live by the new map of life, but the reward would be worth it. Jessie told me he realized, "To obtain true happiness is to give happiness."

Giving happiness to others to gain your own happiness is one of the most life altering lessons anyone can ever learn. Sadly, this lesson is not learned by many people.

I learned a lot of things from Jessie. He only had a high school education, but he was one of the smartest people I have ever talked with. It was impossible to say what he could have become if he had gone to college.

Just like a lot of other people that came from the hood, Jessie was hooked on the crack-pipe and knew he had no future. A Black man, just out of prison for the fourth time, has little chance of succeeding in life. Jessie knew that all too well.

## Chapter 27
## Don Was a Great Cop

Don was a great street cop and the nicest person you would ever want to meet. He made the most felony arrests in the patrol unit because he was a hunter. He had a knack for talking to the hookers and drug dealers in order to get information from them.

They all seemed to like, or at least respect, him. Don never talked down to any street person and mingled with them every day. He knew all the criminals in his area by first name. He had a unique way of talking with them on their own level. Don was the quintessential street cop.

If a burglary or robbery occurred in his area, there was a good chance he would know who committed the crime within several hours of hitting the streets. He would talk to the snitches he'd developed over the years and get the information he wanted. Don gave hundreds of dollars in cigarettes and money to the street informants that gave him good information, which led to many felony arrests of all types.

This was good old fashion police work. It worked well for Don. The street people liked him and wanted to be his friend. They would share information with him because they knew they could trust him. He wouldn't give their names up or say where he got his information because that would likely get them killed.

It's a funny thing, but cops know when they do a good job. An example is when the suspect they just arrested thanks them for being nice and respectful. A lot of cops treat the street people like they were bad. They have no empathy. They think just because the person is a drunken derelict, they have the right to talk down to them. Don was very different; he had people thanking him daily for the way he did his job.

Don liked to drink more than he should have, as many of us did back when we were young cops. Having *choir practice* after work with thirty cops was the norm for several years. We all sat around drinking beer in the department parking lot, talking about the radio calls we handled that night. The sun would soon rise, sending us home to our pissed-off wives.

That's where a lot of us older cops bonded with each other. I'm not sure if that same bond exists in younger cops today. We each got drunk and shared our frustrations about asshole supervisors or the crazy guy we almost had to shoot. We laughed a lot every night at each other's stories and even cried a few times at the unspeakable things we saw.

Words cannot describe what it's like to be first on the scene of some horrible calls.

I was the first to arrive on many such calls. A train once ran over a person lying down on the tracks in a drunken sleep. The body was torn to shreds, scattered for hundreds of yards down the track.

Seeing two young people who just jumped out of a twenty-story building together has always stuck in my mind. Some of the body parts were mixed together, and it was hard to tell them apart.

The poor college student who killed himself because he got bad grades. The young man who made a large pipe bomb and lit the fuse while lying in his bed. He then placed the bomb under his head, at which time it exploded. His brains were scattered around the room, and some were stuck to the walls and ceiling.

It's very hard to tell a non-cop what it's like to experience these horrible calls. Knowing another cop who can relate to you is a very comforting thing. Other cops can understand what you are going through because of their own experiences.

Professional counselors are very helpful to a lot of cops and no doubt have saved many lives. It still is hard for many cops to talk to someone who has never been out of their office, let alone seeing a critical incident unfold in front of them. Many cops feel if you haven't been there, then you don't know what it's like.

One day, I got off duty at five in the morning. I was driving home while listening to my portable police radio. It was standard for me to bring my radio home each night to recharge the battery. There had been no radio traffic for several minutes when a female voice started to scream over the speaker.

It was Don's wife, who worked as a Community Service Officer (CSO) for our department. Each CSO officer was assigned a portable police radio and took them home at the end of shift, so they could also charge their batteries.

Don and his wife had two small girls that were the pride of his life. Unfortunately, Don and his wife were talking about a divorce, which was devastating to him.

He was always happy and many of us had no idea he was having marital problems. I had just seen him several hours earlier at work. He seemed fine and was smiling as usual.

Don's wife again screamed over the radio that she needed help at their house. Don's house was on my way home, so I raced over there as fast as I could. When I arrived, I found Don's wife standing in the driveway with their two daughters.

She explained that she and the girls moved out of their house several days before. Don called her after he got off work that night and they had a big fight over the phone. She then drove over to Don's house and couldn't find him, but did find his gun safe open, with his favorite gun missing.

Don's wife asked me to look for him because she was afraid he was going to hurt himself by the way he was talking. I walked around to the large ranch-style backyard, calling out Don's name.

I saw Don lying on the patio next to a lounge chair. A small gun was in his right hand, and his brains were scattered on the cement. I started to nut up a little bit, saying, "No, no, no, no," over and over again. I even went over and felt for a pulse on Don's neck, even though it was obvious he was dead.

I called for a supervisor on the radio and then walked to the front yard. Don's wife had heard my request for a supervisor over her radio. She knew that the code I used, 926, could only mean Don was dead. How can anyone comfort two small girls who just lost their father? Sometimes there are not enough hugs or kind words that can help.

It hurt me not being able to comfort Don's girls. I could still remember how bad I felt when my dad died in my arms. Finding Don in the backyard was one of those life altering things that affected me forever. I had seen many dead bodies, but never a close friend who just blew his brains out. I had a numb feeling as I drove home, crying the entire way.

Once I walked in the door, my wife instantly knew something was very wrong. I told Lori about Don. She also knew Don from past social events. We hugged and cried at the thought of losing a good friend and a truly nice person. Things like this can't easily be forgotten.

## Chapter 28
## Post-Traumatic Stress Disorder

After I found Don in his backyard with his brains scattered around him, I started having problems. Weeks later, I was continually replaying it over and over again several times a day. I could see every detail as clear as a bell, as if it were just happening for the first time.

The bad thing was once the movie in my head started playing, I couldn't stop it. It had to play it all the way out to the finish. This was driving me crazy. I knew I should talk to someone about this movie in my head, but I thought it would go away with time. It didn't.

The flashbacks became fewer as the years passed. However, at times, some weird thing I see or hear can trigger the episode off again. It's strange to cry out of the blue about something that happened so long ago. The sad emotions are still there, deep inside.

I thought I was crazy for crying about Don and replaying the movie in my head again and again. Bad luck must have followed my life. I could not imagine going through something worse than seeing a dead friend.

This was not the worst thing that happened to me in my career, as I later found out. Years later, another bad thing happened to me, which consumed my daily thoughts. Those two days changed my life forever.

In the 1980s, PTSD, Post Traumatic Stress Disorder, was not taught in police departments. The "DSM" Diagnostic Statistics Manual first recognized it as a disorder in 1980. I had no idea what was going on with me and had never heard of PTSD before.

Back then, PTSD was not a topic people talked about in the police world, and we had no mental health professionals to talk to about our problems. It would be years before we had any training to understand various stress reactions and anything to do with our mental health.

## Chapter 29
## Being a Field Training Officer

In the late 1970s there was no test to become a Patrol Field Training Officer. Field Training Officers, or FTOs, did not have any special rank and didn't get paid any more than a regular patrol officer.

Only the best cops in patrol division were asked by the patrol watch commander to be an FTO. This was a request that most cops didn't turn down. It was a prestigious compliment to be asked by the watch commander to be an FTO, however it was also a career death sentence to say no to him.

After a few years in the department, I had a good reputation and was asked to be an FTO. I soon realized that my main job was to teach young cops how to be safe.

I remembered all too well the lessons I learned from my first FTO. Officer safety was the first and most important thing all cops must think about on their first day on the job. Going home alive after your shift was over was the most critical lesson to learn.

Catching bad guys and responding to calls was not my primary job any longer. Molding new officers into safe, competent co-workers was my first objective. My second trainee was a twenty-one-year-old blond that should have been a model. She was drop dead gorgeous, and every training officer wanted to train her in many ways.

I was never a lady's man and took pride that I never cheated on my wife. Being a little more than ugly didn't help me get many opportunities, which was a good thing for my marriage. I still found it difficult to work with a hard on when training this rookie.

She was always joking around, grabbing my leg at times, while I drove. The poor girl was not doing such a good job at her officer safety and her reports were horrible. I wrote a bad evaluation on her one day and she started to cry. She then leaned over and hugged me, explaining she was having a rough time in training.

The sweet little thing then placed her hand on my thigh, grazing my dick. I jumped a little, at which time she apologized, saying it was an accident. It may have been an accident, so I didn't say anything about it, plus it sure felt good.

I didn't have the heart to wash her out, and the other FTOs apparently felt the same way. She ended up passing her probation and later became a lieutenant. I was very proud I never took advantage of that rookie, but deep down I always regretted not trying have sex with her.

I took great pride in training young officers. Several incidents will always stick with me about my training officer years. Nightly and weekly reports were completed to document the trainee's progression, in case a rookie officer was doing so badly they needed to be terminated. The department would need the written proof of the rookie's daily actions or mistakes in order to wash them out.

## Chapter 30
## B.G.F. Hit Man

One late night, my trainee and I responded to a shooting at a large apartment complex. These apartments were famous for being the home of half the city's criminals. Cops would not conduct traffic stops alone at night in the complex, because we would probably get a bottle thrown at us from the shadows.

On arrival, officers found a sixteen-year-old teenager laying on the grass next to a bicycle. The kid had just been shot in the head, at a point-blank range, with a 12-gauge shotgun. Half his head was missing, with his brains scattered around like hamburger meat.

The sergeant told the officers to conduct a neighborhood canvas in order to find any witnesses. There was no suspect description. Officers had no idea who just shot this kid. I told my trainee to talk to the occupants of one apartment while I talked with the people next door.

I knocked on the door and after a few minutes, a black man dressed in a bathrobe answered. The man's wife and small child were sitting on the staircase dressed in their nightclothes as well. It was apparent they were just awakened. I apologized for the late-night intrusion and explained about the shooting nearby.

The guy said he saw some kids running down the parking lot after he heard a shot, and one was holding a gun. I got descriptions of the possible suspects and made the appropriate broadcast. After taking his statement, I got his driver's license and recorded his name for the report.

The man was very soft-spoken and polite. He offered me a cup of coffee during the interview and appeared well educated. I thanked the family and wrote my report along with my trainee's supplement. The suspects were not caught that shift and I drove home to find my phone ringing.

I answered the phone, wondering who in the hell was calling at three in the morning. It was the homicide sergeant, which got my attention pretty fast. The sergeant explained that they ran a check on my witness, as standard procedure in any homicide. It turned out he was on parole for a triple murder.

The sergeant told me the nice man I talked to was a confirmed "BGF," Black Guerilla Family hit man. He had just got out of prison after doing twenty years for the murders he was involved in. The guy was the driver of the getaway car after his friend killed three people during a drug rip off.

A neighbor of my witness also heard the gunshot and looked out his window. He saw the guy I talked to run to his car and put something long in the trunk. The sergeant said they responded back to the guy's apartment, and a neighbor said the guy and his family had driven away after the police left the complex. The next day, the detectives contacted the suspect's mother and told her to have him turn himself in. Within several hours, the suspect walked into the police station and confessed. He also showed the detectives where he hid the chrome-plated, pistol-gripped, 12-gauge shotgun. It was a hitman's gun, to be sure.

The guy shot the kid because he stole his son's bicycle that same day. I was amazed when I went to court and looked at the suspect. The district attorney was seeking the death penalty, but the suspect sat in his chair as if he didn't have a care in the world. He was calm and appeared happy and content during the trial. I realized he wanted to go back to prison, or at least the prospect of going back didn't bother him.

I was very lucky that night. I did not have any clue or indication the guy had killed someone just minutes earlier. Relaxing and letting my guard down when taking his statement made me an easy target.

## Chapter 31
## They Threw Eggs at My House

One Friday night, I was training another brand-new female officer. She was only out of the academy for two weeks. It was around midnight when we decided to eat at a large coffee shop. The place was packed, but cops always got served fast and got half-price food because we tipped the waitresses well.

My trainee and I had just sat down in our favorite booth at the rear of the restaurant. Four teenagers ran inside the front door, yelling that a man was shooting at them outside. I radioed for help and started walking with my partner towards the double swing wood door.

A teenage Asian girl then slowly opened the front door. A man, about fifty-years-old, walked behind the girl. She stood in front of me with a terrified look on her face. The man was holding a 22 rifle against the girl's back. I screamed at the guy to drop the gun, but he yelled back, "No, they threw eggs at my house."

For the first in my career, I knew that I was about to kill a person. For a split second, I thought of kicking the rifle out of the guy's hands. I then thought that was a crazy idea, which would likely get me killed.

My trainee was standing behind another booth, yelling at the old fart to drop the gun. The young Asian girl then ran behind the cash register, leaving me standing a few feet away from the guy holding a rifle.

I again told the guy to drop the gun. At the same time, I pointed my revolver at the suspect's head and started to squeeze the trigger. The guy must have known he was about to die, because he dropped the gun.

The restaurant was packed, with numerous screaming customers scrambling to hide under their tables during the incident. One old man sat in the booth next to the front door. He held a cup of coffee in his hand during the entire episode, while the guy was holding a rifle just feet away.

After the suspect was handcuffed, the old guy stood and walked up to me. He must have been a former soldier or retired cop. I thought the man was going to give me congratulations for doing such a good job. The fellow looked at me and shook his head, saying, "You should have shot hlm."

Looking back, the man was right. The suspect could have raised the rifle and shot me while I was thinking of playing a hero. I would never hesitate to shoot again, and was later involved in three shootouts of my own.

The suspect's rifle had one shell jammed in the action, preventing it from firing. He was upset at some kids, who he thought threw eggs at his house earlier in the night. The guy was a well-to-do architect who lived in an upscale neighborhood.

He woke up and saw his next-door neighbor's kids leaving in a car. The crazy old guy picked up his ten-shot 22 rifle and chased the kids in his car down the street. The guy fired nine shots at the car while holding the rifle out the window.

He hit the car four times on the bumper and trunk. The kids knew that cops always eat at the same restaurant where we were, so they drove to the front door and ran inside. The suspect also stopped, exited his car, and chased them.

Grabbing the last kid by her hair as she tried to get out of the back seat, the suspect stuck the rifle in her back. He saw our police car in the parking lot and was bringing the girl to us for throwing eggs at his house. In his mind, he had done nothing wrong by shooting at the kids.

My rookie partner and I both learned that cops are never safe while on duty. They can't relax, even at Code-7. That's why we were taught not to sit with our backs to a window or door when we eat.

## Chapter 32
## The K-9 Unit

After being in the police department for six years, I took the test to get in the K-9 unit. I always liked dogs more than people and really wanted to be a K-9 handler. I studied night and day in order to pass the test and get the position. Luckily, I got the job even though I wasn't a good test taker.

In those days, it wasn't which officer scored the best who got the position in the K-9 Unit. It came down to who had the best overall reputation as a street cop. We used to call it a "Mafia Call" because the administration was going to pick who they wanted for the job, regardless of test scores.

I had a long talk with the senior K-9 sergeant on my first night in the Unit. We went to an old coffee shop the sergeant suggested because he knew the waitress very well and the price was always right. I later discovered that other supervisors regularly went to that out-of-the-way coffee shop for the free food and good conversation with the friendly young waitress.

I didn't know anything about the K-9 unit and asked the sergeant what I should expect.

The old cop smiled at me. He said working a patrol dog is without a doubt the best job in the department.

The sergeant said K-9 Officers have the freedom and luxuries that patrol officers don't have. K-9 cops have permission to roam the entire city, picking the hottest calls to go to. K-9 officers were mainly dispatched to burglar alarms and serious crimes in progress. They were not dispatched to report calls, family fights, or car accidents.

Being available to respond to assist patrol officers with vehicle pursuits, attempt felony warrant services, or any other request for a dog was the first priority for the K-9 sergeant.

He asked me if I wanted to work a patrol dog that was crossed trained to smell explosives. I thought that sounded interesting and said, "Yes." Little did I know that meant I would be on the bomb squad as well as working in the K-9 Unit!

I thought that only a nut would work on the bomb squad, but I didn't want to sound like a sissy to the sergeant, who was also the supervisor of the Explosive Ordnance Disposal Unit.

During that first night talk, the K-9 sergeant explained that a dog can search a building or outside area quicker, safer, and more efficiently than a dozen cops. He went on to explain that a well-trained police dog can smell a suspect hiding behind a locked door, on top of a building, or under a house.

He said it is much safer to have a police dog search for armed suspects who are hiding in a backyard, than to have officers sticking their heads in bushes in order to find them. Police dogs have made the job safer for patrol officers by the use of their nose. Without a doubt, police dogs nationwide have saved many police officers' lives.

I soon left for Huntsville, Alabama, which was the home of Redstone, the best bomb school in the world. After five weeks in Alabama, I was glad to get back home. I was getting sick of sweet tea and hush puppies.

When I returned from bomb school, I chose to work from seven at night until five in the morning for the twenty years I worked in the K-9 unit. I liked that shift because I didn't have to go to roll calls, and that's when most of the really hot calls came out. Plus, none of the other K-9 handlers wanted to work those crazy hours.

I had no idea how my life would change because of the things I would later see and do in the K-9 unit. During my first few years, there were only four dogs in the entire K-9 unit.

It takes a lot of experience to find and select a suitable dog to work in a police K-9 unit. It's critical to know how to accurately read a dog's body language while the selection tests are being administered.

At least 90% of the dogs we tested to be in the K-9 unit failed at least one part of the selection process. Our old dog trainer, who was at one time a K-9 handler himself, had many years of dog training experience.

Most dog trainers think their method is the best way to train dogs, and he was no different. We trained his way and did not try to deviate. The proof is in the pudding because he turned out great service dogs.

We were taught to be tough on our dogs and not let them show any aggression towards their handler. If our dogs unnecessarily bit anyone during training, they would be harshly punished in order for it to not happen again. The tactics we used were mandatory and the young handlers didn't question the old trainer's methods of training.

## Stake Out Test

The main test that we used to select a patrol K-9 was called the "Stake out Test". This test washed out most potential police dog candidates. This test was easy to perform and most of the time the dog's body language was easy to recognize.

We would ask the owner to take their dog to a local park or a safe remote location that the dog was not familiar with if possible. Once at the location a thirty foot tracking lead would be attached to the dog's collar. He then would be tied of to a fence or tree. The owner along with the K-9 trainer would hide completely out of sight from the dog.

Part 1. Of the test is to watch the dog to see how he acclimates to his new environment. Does he just lay in one spot or does he walk around exploring the territory. Most dogs bark and watch for their owners to return.

Part 2. After the dog settles down an experienced police K-9 agitator makes the first of three walks by the dog. During the first walk by, the agitator stays 30 feet away from the dog and does not make any eye contact with him. The idea is to not put any stress on the dog and see how he reacts to someone walking by.

Some dogs would run the other way just because the agitator walked by them. This would be an obvious fail. Reading how the dog held his ground or even how the dog barked was important. Barking or growling is often a sign of fear or stress which could result in failure.

Part 3. After waiting several minutes out of sight the agitator would make a second pass by the dog. This time he would walk closer and make direct eye contact or stare at the dog while he walks by.

This should cause the dog to react to the threat posed by the agitator. A good reaction would be for the dog to come all the way out to the end of the 30 foot lead in order to bite the agitator.

This almost never occurred with a dog with no attack training. Most dogs would fail during the second pass because they would walk away from the agitator, often with their hair raised up on their backs.

Part 4. The last part of the stake out test was only given to the few dogs that showed any potential during the first stages. Most dogs tested would have been rejected very early on for obvious bad body language.

The agitator would hold a bite sleeve concealed under an old coat while he walks closely past the dog, making heavy eye contact with him. A dog that comes out and tries to bite the agitator is a pass however this was rarely done.

If a dog shows good body language and holds his ground when the agitator tries to make him run away would be a pass, even thou the dog didn't try to bite the agitator. What is important is that the dog shows no fear and holds his ground during the test.

Environmental tests were also tests administered, such as walking the dogs on a slick floor and taking them up a high staircase. These tests washed out unsuitable police dogs after several training attempts to resolve the individual problems failed.

It took three months to fully train our new dogs. The training consisted of obedience, agility and attack training. My dog was also trained for explosive detection.

After the first month of basic training, we started to train our dogs to find people hiding. We started with short inside buildings searches, and later progressed to various outside area searches.

We trained all the time. It was important for our police dogs to learn how to jump over a six foot fence or through a car window during agility training. The dogs would later be expected to do these things on command during real street searches.

During attack training the police dogs were trained to bite people when given the command to do so. Training a dog to bite people was the easy part, making them stop biting and let go of their prey was another story.

At the end of our three month training our dogs were expected to immediately stop biting any suspect when given the command to "out" which meant stop biting. This didn't always happen on the streets for one reason or another.

Our trainer was a stickler for obedience training. We trained our dogs in obedience training every night for thirty minutes. He said obedience was the ground work for all other dog training.

Most K-9 handlers get bit at one time or another while training. It's just the hazards of being in the K-9 Unit. During the first few months of training there were occasionally dog fights and more than one handler got bit.

My best friend in the K-9 Unit, "Don," was watching me do obedience training with my new dog named "Luke," the first week I got him. I knew this dog was very aggressive because he already tried to bite me several times at home the first day I had him.

I didn't know how to correct the problem. I later found out in the first day of training how to correct my dog after he tried to bite me again. Hanging the dog completely off the ground by his leash for several minutes sounded cruel, however, it was an extremely effective technique.

This was the hardest correction we did, and only on the particular dogs that bit their handlers or started dog fights during training. Lifting the dog off the ground by his collar looks abusive, however it causes no physical injury to the dog.

If the technique is done correctly, the dog should correlate the unpleasant experience of being hung off the ground and thinking they're going to die for dog fighting or biting the handler, and neither should happen again.

Don laughed at me because I was wearing a thick pair of my father-in-law's welding gloves when I was doing my obedience training. My dog had bitten my hand when I did a small leash correction the first day of training and I wanted protection.

Don then grabbed the leash out of my hand and told me "He would show me how to handle a hard dog." I warned him not to pull on his leash too hard because he would get bit.

The old trainer, who was standing next to me said, "Can't say you didn't warn him." Don took two steps forward and made a sharp right turn. He then made a bad mistake and gave a good hard tug on the dog's leash.

In a split second, my dog bit Don's right hand to the bone. Don screamed in pain while he was getting bitten. It was a full mouth dog bite, which lasted several seconds, until my dog let go of his hand.

I grabbed the leash from Don, and took my dog to my K-9 vehicle. Don held his hand, which now was bleeding profusely on the pavement. He then stared at me and the trainer and said "don't even say it."

I knew he was in pain but couldn't help myself. While laughing at his unfortunate situation, I had to say "I told you so." Don also smiled, because he knew it was his own fault.

The old trainer laughed for several minutes. He knew it hurt like hell, because he had been bitten dozens of times during training over the years. He also knew that Don learned not to mess with another handler's dog after being warned.

Over the years, numerous freak, unusual, and funny things happened during training. It wasn't fun getting bitten, and I did everything I could to prevent it from happening to me.

I saw a lot of police handlers and their dogs come and go in my 20 years in the K-9 Unit. Some dogs stuck out more than others for various reasons. My dogs always seemed to cause more injuries to suspects than the other dogs in the Unit.

My dog and I soon had the same type of well-deserved nasty reputation. We both liked to use force during arrests. My use of force techniques was always by the book. Want to buy the London Bridge?

I was lucky to have two great police dogs that were very aggressive, and loved to go to work and bite the shit bad guys. The old trainer used to say police dogs often pick up on their handler's emotions. He called it "running down the leash." Most of the other K-9 handlers knew he was right.

One small Rottweiler, named Mouse, was one of the coolest dogs in our department. He only weighed sixty pounds and was the nicest dog you would ever want to play with.

He loved to be petted by anyone, and chasing a ball was his favorite pastime. It was impossible to imagine him being suitable for police work, seeing how nice and playful the dog was.

He was a great police dog because you could turn him on and off like a light switch. Once the dog's handler gave him the command to find or bite someone during training or on the street, the dog became a creature from hell.

He would let out a scary howling sound and turned into a devil dog. He became a searching machine with only one thing in his mind, "find and bite." I saw Mouse bite an auto theft suspect who was hiding in a back yard for less than two seconds.

The handler and I couldn't see the dog in the bushes during the dog's contact with the suspect, and didn't know where he was bitten. After the suspect was transported to the hospital emergency ward in a code three ambulance, we found out his right eye was taken out during the dog bite.

The dog's handler always felt guilty about the severe injury his dog caused during that arrest. Years later, he talked to me about it and started to cry. He left the K-9 Unit only after a few years and returned to patrol until he retired.

It took a special type of person to work a police dog. Some K-9 handlers seldom saw much action because they were afraid their dogs might get hurt during deployment.

It is easy to become too attached to your K-9 partner and forget that he is a very important tool to be used when called for. No handler anywhere wants to see their dog get hurt.

It's a sad fact that a good K-9 handler must accept that when it comes down to it, "it's better to have their dog get shot than another cop." A K-9 handler must be able to sacrifice their beloved friend, family member and partner for another cop's life, if called for in an emergency.

Most K-9 Officers only handled one dog before leaving the Unit. Many handlers with good reputations got promoted to sergeant straight out of the K-9 Unit. Their street experience made them a valuable commodity to the department.

K-9 cops usually took charge in pursuits and during crimes in progress. Having a good reputation as a hard worker in the K-9 Unit is one of the best stepping stones for promotion to Sergeant in any police department in the country.

Now I know why being in the K-9 Unit is without a doubt the best job in the department. Playing with my dog during training and then handling only the most exciting calls throughout the city made it fun to come to work each night. Handling hot calls soon became an addiction that lasted many years.

## Chapter 33
## Basic Rules

After a few years in the K-9 unit, I started teaching patrol officers search procedures and tactics. One thing I used to teach officers was to stay where they were after losing sight of the suspect in a foot pursuit.

I instructed officers to "stay put" and "listen" for a few seconds for the sounds of fences being jumped or the suspect moving around, before they started talking on the radio and setting up a perimeter. Most suspects will hide very close, sometimes just feet from where they were last seen running.

One day shift, a California Highway Patrol officer was in a high-speed vehicle pursuit with a stolen car on the freeway. The stolen car left the expressway and entered the city limits, with the CHP officer right behind him. Seconds later, the vehicle was found by the lead CHP officer abandoned on the front lawn of a large residence, with the driver's door wide open.

The officer was right behind the stolen car when he found it abandoned. He set up a perimeter of officers around the block where the suspect ran and requested a city K-9 team to assist with a search.

A city K-9 officer arrived on the scene to conduct an area search. The K-9 handler contacted the CHP officer, who had his clipboard lying on the hood of the stolen vehicle.

He was writing out a recovery form and told the K-9 cop the suspect must have run in the backyard. The handler told the CHP officer to back away from the stolen car because he was going to start the search where the suspect was last known to be—in the driver's seat.

The CHP officer grabbed his clipboard off the hood and walked to his squad car before the K-9 officer started his search. He learned an important lesson that day.

The police dog dove under the front of the stolen car and started biting the suspect, who began screaming out of pain. Surprised, the CHP officer started to run up and look under the car when the K-9 officer stopped him.

The K-9 officer gave his dog the command to stop biting and return to his side, which he did. He then ordered the suspect to show his hands and crawl out from under the car or he would be bitten again.

The suspect complied, and was handcuffed and taken into custody by the CHP officer, who then got the shock of his life. He looked under the car and found a fully loaded 357 Magnum.

Apparently, the suspect rolled under the car armed with a handgun after the pursuit ended. The CHP officer had been standing over the armed suspect for fifteen minutes while doing his paperwork.

## Chapter 34
## Hide and Seek

Sometimes I would be the only K-9 handler working in the entire city and would respond to one felony call after another. Being in several high-speed pursuits each night during the summer was a normal occurrence.

In the old days, the graveyard watch commanders seldom, if ever, called out the SWAT team for any major call, even though they probably should have. They often relied on me and my dog to handle dangerous calls, like crawling under a house or in an attic to arrest a felony suspect.

Vehicle pursuits were a big part of my career. K-9 units were sent to respond to all pursuits in the city, because most ended with the suspect running from the vehicle. Using a police dog is the safest and most efficient way to apprehend a fleeing suspect.

K-9 units were trained to be the number one car following behind the suspect's vehicle during pursuits, in case the suspect flees on foot once the pursuit ends. This way, the patrol dog has the shortest distance to cover to chase down the fleeing suspect. Plus, the dog does not have to run past any patrol officers, preventing accidental dog bites.

K-9 officers don't like to talk on their car radios during pursuits, because their dogs bark too much. I always loved being the first car in vehicle pursuits, because they were always so exciting.

One of my favorite pastimes was to look for occupied, stolen vehicles driving around the city. When located, the stolen vehicles wouldn't stop and a pursuit would ensue, ending in a dog deployment, and a "dog bite."

During the late-night hours, patrol officers would often find unoccupied stolen cars parked in bad neighborhoods. The patrol cops would park a block away and spot on the hot car until the crook would come back to the car and drive away.

This was common for me to do for many years, resulting in a lot of pursuits and many dog bites. At times, the patrol cops would get a radio call before anyone came back to the unoccupied parked stolen car.

They would just leave it there and come back later in the shift to recover and tow the car. Many times, when they returned later in their shift, they would find the car was missing, which meant it was driving around in the area.

The cops would then call me to come to look for the stolen vehicle. This was like a game of Hide and Seek. That late at night, very few cars were driving around, besides cops and crooks. I was soon chasing down every taillight I saw in the neighborhood.

It may sound sadistic and not very politically correct, but seeing a police dog jump out of a K-9 unit's rear window and chase down a felony suspect, who just ran from a car, is like poetry in motion to a K-9 cop.

Seeing your dog chase down and bite a suspect after a vehicle pursuit or after he finds someone hiding during a building search makes all the countless hours of daily training worth it.

The practice of not recovering stolen vehicles when found unoccupied later stopped. Police Administrators found out a couple of high-speed pursuits that ended in fatalities could have been avoided if the unoccupied stolen cars were recovered when found. A policy change soon followed. My late-night game of Hide and Seek ended. Or did it?

## Chapter 35
## Pursuit Immobilization Technique

Chasing after a five-thousand-pound car during a police vehicle pursuit has always been one of the most dangerous things cops do. The unpredictability of how a suspect drives often puts the officer and the public in extreme danger.

Each year, hundreds of innocent lives are lost during high-speed police vehicle pursuits throughout our country. Stopping these treacherous pursuits as fast as possible is the best way to protect the public and save lives.

Things never stay the same in police work. Years after I came on the department, cops were trained in the P.I.T, "Pursuit Immobilization Technique," which spun the suspect car out, causing the engine to die. If done correctly, this simple technique can put an end to a dangerous vehicle pursuit.

This maneuver is done while driving at a relatively slow speed below 45 MPH. The police car should pull alongside the suspect vehicle so the front quarter panel of the squad car would be next to the rear wheels of the suspect vehicle.

Once the front tires of the squad car are as close as possible to the rear of the suspect vehicle, the officer makes a smooth sharp turn directly into the rear quarter panel and accelerates the police car in a straight line without slowing down. The suspect vehicle should spin out in a half circle, often causing the engine to die. The second unit in the pursuit should then position their squad car in front of the suspect vehicle, who should be facing their direction from the spin out.

Often, suspects put their cars in reverse and the pursuit continues. The PIT maneuver works well on suspect vehicles which have had their tires flattened by police spike stripes.

Spike stripes are often used to deflate the suspect vehicle tires. Cops have been killed and injured while throwing spikes in front of the moving suspect vehicles. Officers must use these tools and techniques in the way they were trained in order to make the job safer for them and the public.

K-9 officers would drop back to the number two position just prior to a PIT maneuver being deployed by another unit. K-9 cops usually didn't deploy the PIT maneuver in their K-9 units.

Often when deploying the PIT maneuver, the police vehicle sustains minimal body damage. The K-9 unit didn't have many spare

K-9 cars to use if one was getting body work after a PIT.

K-9 cops wanted to be second in line after a PIT, because suspects often bailed out of the car once it spun out. The police dog could then have a clear shot at the fleeing suspect without other cops getting in the way.

This was called a direct send out of the K-9 unit's rear window. Watching my dog knock a suspect off his feet as he tried to run away was pure elegance to me. It is also the safest way to stop a fleeing criminal.

Mike and first patrol K-9, Bear in 1986 during training at a city parking garage in downtown Sacramento.

Bear was Mike's partner for seven years until his hips started giving him problems. He found and bit over one hundred suspects. Getting a street bite was considered a positive status symbol in the K-9 unit. Mike was always #1 or #2 in the unit for the bites his dogs got.

This continued with Mike's second patrol dog, Luke, who worked the streets for an incredible twelve years. Luke found and bit over two hundred suspects, and was considered a very aggressive dog.

## Chapter 36
## High Find

One late night, a suspect robbed a 7-11 convenience store at gunpoint, then got away in a stolen car. A patrol officer located the vehicle a short distance away, and another high-speed pursuit ensued in a residential neighborhood.

After several minutes of multiple right and left turns, the suspect crashed his vehicle into a parked car. He jumped out of the moving car, which he left in drive, and vaulted over a fence. The driverless vehicle continued forward until it hit another parked car.

A large two block perimeter was established around the location where the suspect was last seen. After an hour-long search, the sector sergeant asked me if my dog was getting any alerts. The radio calls were backing up, and he was going to have to cut some perimeter units loose to handle the priority calls that were pending.

My dog had not shown any interest in any areas during my yard search, so I told the sergeant he could C-4, or cancel the perimeter, which he did. I told the patrol sergeant that I was going to continue to search outside the perimeter for a few minutes.

I took another K-9 handler with me as a cover officer. It was not very safe for me to do, but I rarely took any patrol officers with me while I conducted any area or building search.

Most patrol officers didn't know how to cover a K-9 officer during a yard or building search. Patrol cops would often start walking around and looking on their own for the suspect, while the police dog was searching the same backyard.

Patrol cops who cover a K-9 officer should remain close to the K-9 handler during the search. This is to prevent them from getting bitten and to provide the K-9 officer with needed cover while he moves around.

During searches, K-9 officers closely watch their dogs for any changes in their body language, which would indicate the suspect's location. At times, the K-9 officer must follow their dog without using any cover, such as a wall or solid object, for protection. It's at these times, the cover officer must pay attention to the K-9 officer's movements and not be looking around on their own.

Sometimes we used two dogs to conduct a search. When there were multiple suspects who fled, or when the area or building was too large for one dog to search, two K-9's were often used at different locations.

This night, the search area was small and only one dog was needed. It was a calm summer evening, and the conditions were perfect for the dog to find the suspect quickly. My dog had his faults, but he was great at finding and biting suspects. This was the most important thing for me to know he could do.

Police dogs were just like police officers. They all had their own distinct personalities, special abilities, and funny quirks. Some dogs had amazing obedience.

On another occasion, an additional K-9 unit arrived at a large department store to help me look for several suspects who had been seen running around inside by a security officer. After talking for a couple of minutes, the K-9 officer went to get his dog out of his car.

He opened the rear door to his K-9 Unit only to find it was empty. His dog was gone. The handler said, "Shit," jumped into his car, and sped away. He returned in fifteen minutes and told us the story.

Just before he first responded to help with the building search, he stopped off at a city park to let his dog go to the bathroom. He was in a hurry and thought his dog jumped back into the rear of the Unit before he went to help with the search.

The Handler said when he returned to the park where he left his bewildered partner, he found him lying exactly where he left him. His dog won numerous awards at different police dog trials for obedience.

My dog would have not stayed for long if I left him in a park. My dog had one serious problem, which I had to watch out for all the time. He hated other dogs and would start a fight for no reason at all. This was a big problem during searches. On more than one occasion, he got into a fight with another police dog.

The only thing that worked to stop his aggressive behavior was to work him with an electric shock collar. This tool is commonly used today in many K-9 Units throughout the country. Corrections can be given at greater distances, which are hard to duplicate with other tactics or methods of K-9 training.

During this search for the robbery suspect, I took a veteran K-9 officer who I could trust. After searching three or four homes, my dog started to show interest in a large two-story shed in the rear of a large backyard.

My dog's head was raised high, and his tail was sticking straight up in the air. He pranced around, looking up at the roof of the shed. It didn't take a rocket scientist to see he was alerting to the roof. The other K-9 handler and I both knew the suspect was up there.

The suspect could jump down on the other side of the shed if he wanted to run away and hide again. Getting him to come down without causing him to run away was going to take some imagination.

I told the other handler, in a loud voice, that my dog was not picking up on anything and we should go to dinner. The suspect could hear me and hopefully fall for my plan.

I then whispered to the handler to walk out the gate and go to the back side of the shed and hide. I told him I was going to walk out the gate, then jump the far fence with my dog back into the rear-yard and hide in the bushes until the suspect came down from the roof on his own.

After the other handler and I were hiding in some bushes for about thirty minutes, I saw the suspect peek his head up from the roof and look around. I couldn't use my radio because he was climbing down only a few feet away from where I was hiding.

Once he stepped into the backyard, I gave him one last chance to give up and lie down. The suspect was not too smart and thought he was faster than a dog. He took one step to run, when I ordered my dog to stop him. After his second step, he was screaming in pain from being bitten on his lower leg.

The other handler jumped the fence and handcuffed the suspect, at which time an ambulance was called for his injuries. Most dog bites caused puncture wounds which just needed to be cleaned after the bite. My dog liked to shake his head while biting, causing the skin to rip and tear. This required the suspects to get stitched up at the hospital.

Mike with Bear on a leash during training in downtown Sacramento in 1987.

## Chapter 37
## The Bond

I want to share an unbelievable relationship between a man and his dog. If you have ever looked into a dog's eyes and wondered if they knew what you were thinking, then you will understand this story.

Have you ever met someone who you liked instantly? People with such magnetic charisma are a rare breed indeed. This story is how one such person touched the lives of so many.

After reading this, you may agree that there is much more out in the world that meets the eye. Our imagination is the only thing that limits our ability to understand the unknown.

For a few years, I had the pleasure of working around another K-9 officer named Denny. He was an extremely happy person, who had a beautiful wife named Sara. They had a small son named Will, who loved his dad's police dog named Leo.

Leo was like Will's big brother, and they played together every day in the backyard. Leo was a two-year-old, black and tan German shepherd. He had one of the strongest bites in the K-9 unit and bit numerous felony suspects during his career.

He was very friendly and had a great personality, which allowed Denny to take him to any grade school and let the kids all pet him. Denny and Leo were the ideal team.

One month, Denny had a persistent cough that wouldn't go away. His cough was getting worse, so he went to the doctor to get some antibiotics for the damn cold that was hanging on for so long.

The doctor examined Denny and did the usual blood tests on him, like so many times before in his life. Later, the doctor called Denny into his office, which was a bit unusual.

Denny was more than apprehensive when the doctor asked him to sit down. He received the news like a punch in the mouth. Denny was told he had cancer.

To make things worse, he had just found out two days before that his wife was pregnant. His mind was spinning with thoughts of what the doctor had just told him.

Denny never had a doubt that he was going to beat his cancer, not just for him, but for Sara, Will, and their unborn child. They needed him and there was no way he was going to lose the fight of his life. Cancer treatment robs dignity and kills the will to live in some, but not in Denny. He was the epitome of bravery.

Anyone who has stayed in the hospital can tell you it can be one scary place to wake up in.

Denny had the will to do whatever it would take to beat his cancer. His extended family from the K-9 unit and the rest of the department came to visit him and give their best wishes.

I remember leaving the hospital with an empty feeling that I could do nothing to help a friend that was dying, other than to pray. People have strength in numbers, and it is not truer than in a common prayer. "Please God, let Denny get well."

Denny completed the grueling chemo and radiation therapy. I think he was the first officer to set the trend for having a bald head. It wasn't long afterwards most of the young officers in our department had heads as smooth as billiard balls.

To every one's surprise, Denny did beat his cancer. His wife gave birth to a baby boy, and life was looking a lot better for him. Leo loved playing in the backyard with Will every day during his long sabbatical, but he was more than ready to go back to work. Soon Denny and Leo were chasing down bad guys, liked they both loved to do.

Denny loved working a police dog more than anything else he had ever done in his career. They worked as a team for several more years. Denny and Leo always had a rare bond between them, unlike other K-9 teams.

Working as a team with a police dog becomes part of your life; it's much more than just a job. An officer's family is also attached to the dog as a family member. A dog has the innocence of a small child, who gives you unconditional love, with no prejudice or hatred. I think you can see God in a dog's eyes. Maybe I am crazy and just spelled dog backwards too many times.

When I was a young boy, my dad taught me that "time and change" are the only things which are truly absolute in this world. Denny knew this also and took the sergeant's test for a promotion. He loved working with Leo, but he was getting older, and nothing stays the same.

Denny scored very high on the sergeant's test and was promoted in a few weeks. On his last night, working as a K-9 officer, Denny was about to leave for work when he noticed his son, Will, was crying.

Will told his dad that he was crying because he would never see Leo again. Will thought his dad was going to have to turn Leo into the department with his K-9 vehicle. Little kids get weird ideas like this, from only God knows where.

Denny told Will that Leo would be part of their family for the rest of his life, and they would never get rid of him. It was department policy that the K-9 handlers got to keep their dogs if they worked them over five years, which Denny had done.

Will's face lit up like a Christmas tree, at which time he gave Leo the biggest hug of his life. Denny told Will that he would see Leo in the morning when he got home. Will hugged Leo one more time, as his head hung out the police car's rear window, like he did every day before work.

After a few hours at work, Denny noticed Leo becoming lethargic. Leo had not been his usual self the last several days, but dogs get that way sometimes. Leo continued to look worse during the shift, so Denny took him to the emergency veterinary clinic that was used by the K-9 unit.

After the examination and X-rays, the doctor told Denny that Leo had advanced terminal cancer and was in extreme pain. Denny didn't want any further suffering, so he made the toughest decision in his life. He asked that his four-legged friend and partner be put to sleep.

He called his family to give them the bad news. His family drove to the hospital to say goodbye to Leo. There wasn't a dry eye in the office when Will gave Leo a hug for the last time. It was hard to say goodbye through all the tears, but the memories will live forever. Denny stroked his dog's head one more time and then it was over. Leo was gone from this world.

It's very sad to think such a kind man and loving family lost a family member. Denny's son would only get to play with Leo in his dreams. A police department lost a friend who lived to protect his larger family in blue.

I think the world holds mysteries that are not understood. The bond between a dog and a person may be more than a strong emotional attachment. Was it just a mere coincidence that Leo died during his last shift with Denny?

How could a police dog know he was going to die and stay alive until his last shift? Some things we may never know until our individual time is right. Can it be possible that a bond between a person and a dog can exist in some unknown physical way?

Science has discovered that dogs can smell cancer cells in the human body. We have long known the calming effects and healing potential animals have on the elderly. Some animals have been considered gods in many other cultures.

Maybe through some evolutionary process, animals have adapted to mankind and gained the power to heal. I wonder if a bond can be strong enough that an animal can take cancer or other illnesses away from a human.

When some sick people live or die, given the same set of circumstances, is it divine intervention or canine intervention? I know this sounds preposterous, but sending a man to the moon was thought to be impossible not too long ago.

The wonders of our medical marvels are just beginning to be explored and understood. At some time in the future, will we look back and be puzzled about why the healing properties of animals were overlooked for so long? Life is a true mystery; however, all our questions will be answered when the time is right.

Mike and Bear next to trophies they won at their first dog trial. Bear was not a very good trial dog, but he was a great street dog who loved his job almost as much as Mike did.

## Chapter 38
## K-9 Church Search

I loved working in the K-9 unit. This was the best job in the department for a sadistic cop, who liked animals more than people. Nothing was more fun than seeing a police dog find and bite the hell out of some shit bag who had just robbed some old lady of her purse. Many times, suspects have kicked some poor old lady in the head, who just tried to hang onto to her belongings.

I liked working by myself at night so I could get all the good K-9 calls in the entire city. One night, a guy was shot inside the city. The only other K-9 working was from the sheriff's department. The search area was very large, and two dogs were needed. I asked the county K-9 unit for his help.

After the search, I met up with the county K-9 handler and asked him if his dog got any alerts. The handler told me his dog got a small alert behind the church on the opposite side of the street, but he didn't find anything.

All the patrol units were canceled, and I thanked the county canine officer for helping me. Most K-9 handlers think their dog is the best in the world and I was no different. I thought maybe the county K-9 handler's dog might have missed the suspect behind the church, so I would give it a second sweep.

I had just started my search when my dog Luke ran into some bushes behind the church. There was no mistake from the dog's body language and his alerts that a suspect was in the bushes.

In a few seconds, I heard the common blood-curdling scream of a suspect being bitten by my dog. I felt great finding the bad guy after the county dog missed him.

I gave Luke the command to stop biting and return to my side, which he did. The suspect then walked out of the bushes holding his right arm, which was freshly bandaged.

I could see this guy was an obvious transient by the way he was dressed and the sleeping bag by his feet. He then screamed, "You asshole, your dog just bit me fifteen minutes ago." He was holding his right arm, which had fresh blood seeping through a gauze bandage.

The guy continued to tell me what an asshole I was for letting my dog bite him twice. Then he saw I was not the same K-9 unit. The transient asked me, "Don't you f--king cops talk to each other?"

I realized the county K-9 officer's dog had bitten the innocent guy who was sleeping under a tree. He bandaged his arm with a roll of gauze and didn't tell anyone about the bite.

My dog found the guy and bit him on the same arm. This poor transient was accidentally bitten twice in fifteen minutes by two different police dogs.

This guy now needed a code three ambulance for severe bleeding and shock. I called my watch commander and explained the bullshit pulled on me. My watch commander phoned the county watch commander, who said he would make some inquires.

In ten minutes, the county watch commander called back. He contacted the involved county K-9 officer. That officer said he was writing an accidental bite report and was going to tell his K-9 sergeant about the incident at the end of the watch. That K-9 officer later became a sergeant and then a lieutenant.

Bear jumping out the rear window of a K-9 Unit. The rear windows were always down on radio calls in case we needed to call the dogs when we were away from the car.

Our dogs were trained never to jump out of the car unless called. They were also trained never to bite anyone from the car. Unfortunately, several officers were bitten by other handlers' dogs when they ran by an open rear window of a K-9 unit. This was always a hazard of working around dogs. Accidental bites to officers and innocent civilians happened from time to time.

Now days K-9 units have screens over their rear windows and the doors have automatic openers which are controlled remotely by the door open switch worn on the handler's belt. This prevents the dogs biting from the car.

## Chapter 39
## My Dog Saved My Life

One late night, a security guard called the police to report a burglary in progress at a mortuary. The security guard stated he lived upstairs above the mortuary and heard some glass breaking, then someone moving around downstairs.

The watchman was correct. A suspect, fresh out of prison for only a few days, stole a car from another mortuary in Los Angeles where he sexually abused several dead bodies. The suspect drove hundreds of miles to another mortuary in our city. He was going to steal another car, not knowing a security guard lived upstairs.

Numerous officers responded to the burglary in progress. They found a broken window in the rear of the business and the suspect's stolen car in the parking lot. The officers established a perimeter around the building and called for a K-9 unit because a dog would be needed to search the inside.

I arrived with my dog, Bear, to conduct the building search. I gave the required verbal warning, for "Anyone inside to come out or you'll be bitten by a police dog." After repeating the admonishment and receiving no response, I started my search, as I had done hundreds of times before.

I didn't like bringing other officers with me during searches because they would get in my dog's way. Plus, they would be one more witness I would have to worry about if something went wrong.

I entered the main business office and saw a large oak desk. I noticed that it had been pried open. This desk had three drawers on each side and one middle drawer. Five out of the six drawers were pried open, with their contents spread on the floor. The sixth drawer had pry marks around the lock, but it was still secure.

A small shower room with a walk-in closet was next to the office. I entered the tiny dark room and slid open the walk-in closet door. To my surprise, the suspect was standing just inside the closet. I only had my flashlight on and could not see the guy's hands.

The guy swung his left hand in a sideways motion towards my chest. Bear jumped up and grabbed the suspect's forearm and began biting him. Bear was a good police dog that loved to bite bad guys.

I shined my flashlight on the suspect and saw he was holding a large sixteen-inch hunting knife in his left hand. This type of knife was the outdoor survival type, with a compass in the handle and a serrated blade.

I then realized this asshole just tried to kill me. The guy was bent over and still holding the knife, while being bitten by my dog. I stepped back and kicked him in the head as hard as I could. It was either kicking him or shooting him, which would have resulted in his quick death.

The suspect dropped the knife and was handcuffed. I looked my dog over because I thought he must have been stabbed during the confrontation. The dog apparently hung onto the guy's left arm during the fight. The suspect didn't have a chance to use his knife on me or my dog.

My dog and I were not hurt during the life and death confrontation. The suspect sustained a few minor injuries. He had a broken left forearm from the dog bite, a fractured cheek bone and several broken front teeth. He was later found guilty of the attempted murder of a police officer and several other felonies.

Once the owner of the mortuary arrived on the scene, I got the scare of my life. I had come closer to being killed than I thought. The owner and I stood in his office around the large oak desk that the suspect pried open. He told me it was a miracle the suspect didn't get all the way into the last drawer.

He then removed his keys from his pocket, unlocked the drawer, and opened it. I was stunned when I saw a six-inch revolver lying on top of some papers. I then realized how close I came to dying that night.

If the suspect was crazy enough to try to stab me, he would not have hesitated to shoot me. It was my good fortune and pure luck he tried to pry open the drawer with a loaded gun in it last.

Police work is a lot about luck. My first experience with an officer in our department who died on duty was a freak accident. The rookie officer was getting dressed for work in the locker room before roll call. He was in the process of placing his six-shot revolver in his locker when it must have slipped out of his hands.

Investigators surmised he tried to grab the falling gun and accidentally pulled the trigger, firing the gun into his head, killing him instantly. Numerous officers ran to give aid, but it was obvious he was dead. He left a wife and two small children. Sometimes life is just not fair.

## Chapter 40
## My Own Dog Bit Me

One late night, I was listening to a high-speed pursuit on my scanner. The pursuit was headed my way, and the suspect was a wanted parolee driving a stolen car. It wasn't long before I saw the line of flashing squad cars chasing the bad guy.

The suspect turned his headlights off and blew through a red light at a 100 miles per hour. This guy was driving like a madman and had to be stopped. These types of pursuits often ended in tragedy, where an innocent person is hurt or killed, and the suspect isn't even scratched.

I soon took the lead in the pursuit in case the suspect fled on foot. I could now send my dog to stop the suspect without the fear of an officer running in his path and getting bitten.

After a few wild turns, the bad guy crashed his car and took off running down the street. Once the guy stepped out of the car, I knew I might have trouble with the arrest.

The suspect stood six feet, five inches and weighed 250 pounds, all of which was muscle. In other words, it looked like a brick shithouse running down the street, as fast a rabbit.

I gave my dog, Luke, the order to stop the fleeing suspect. This, of course, meant the dog would have to run him down and bite him. It was a beautiful thing to see my police dog jump out of the K-9 unit's rear window and start running after this monster of a man.

Luke had a reputation of being a very aggressive dog when it came to biting suspects. Most of his dog bites resulted in the suspects receiving numerous stitches from gaping wounds. He was the last dog you would want chasing your ass down the street. He loved his job almost as much as I did.

Once Luke caught up with the running bad guy, he jumped up like a rocket and struck the guy in the back, knocking him to the ground. I was still running about twenty yards behind, because I was not as fast as the dog or suspect.

To my amazement, the suspect stood up and picked the dog up off the ground by the throat with one hand. He then began punching the dog in the face with his fist. Luke continued to bite at the punches being thrown at him.

I wasn't the toughest guy in the world, but I played four years as a middle linebacker on my high school football team. Seeing my dog being punched made me more than a little upset.

Running at full speed, I made the best tackle of my life. Of course, the suspect had his back turned to me when I made contact, but it was still a great hit. This was going to be a good fight. I was sure glad I had a dog on my side.

Once we landed on the ground, the fight was on. Both the suspect and I were punching each other while rolling on the ground. Luke was now biting us both. He was not a mean dog, but during the struggle on the ground, he didn't know which one was the bad guy.

Since he loved to bite, he bit both of us several times each. My dog really didn't care who he bit, as long as he got to sink his teeth into someone. Some dogs bite to please their handlers; Luke bit because he liked it.

At one point, I felt a tremendous tugging on my right lower leg. At first, I thought it was someone trying to pull me off the suspect. I looked down and saw my dog had a full mouth bite on my right calf.

He was now shaking his head from side to side, tearing my leg wide open. Several officers now ran up to the fight. I rolled off the suspect and grabbed my dog, so they wouldn't get bit as well.

Four officers were hitting the suspect with their batons and using pepper spray in an attempt to subdue the crazy giant. The suspect was not going down at all. The baton blows and pepper spray had no effect on him.

It was extremely lucky that our department's strongest and toughest cop ran up to the violent fight. John was not a big cop, but he didn't have an ounce of fat on him. He worked out for several hours every day.

John grabbed the suspect around the neck during the struggle. He later testified that he was attempting to perform a carotid restriction hold, to render the suspect unconscious.

This technique is used to squeeze the carotid arteries on both sides of the neck. This cuts off the oxygenated blood from reaching the brain. If done properly, the suspect should go unconscious for about ten seconds, with no lasting injury.

While John and the others were struggling with the suspect, I limped over to my car and put Luke inside the rear seat. I looked down at my leg and only saw a small tear in my pants. It was then that I saw tiny pieces of fatty tissues on my pants and knew that wasn't a good sign.

It was a funny thing. Up to that point, I had not felt any pain at all because of the adrenalin rush of the fight. I sat on a curb, not knowing how badly I was hurt. I then pulled my pant leg up and almost puked when I saw my mangled leg.

The dog bite caused several gaping wounds on both sides of my right calf. Luke had a great full mouth. The pain now hit me like a ton of bricks and a code three ambulance was requested.

I was losing a lot of blood, and the pain was horrible. Once the ambulance arrived, I was helped into the back and onto the gurney. Once inside, I put a towel in my mouth to bite down on it because of the pain. It later took thirty stitches to close my wounds. This was one of Luke's better bites.

Before the ambulance left, another K-9 officer poked his head in the rear to talk to me. He said the fire department was doing CPR on the suspect, who looked like he was dead. I thought the officer was joking and looked out the window as we were driving away. Sure enough, the fire department paramedic was performing CPR on the suspect.

At first, I thought I or my dog had killed the guy during the violent struggle. I'd thrown many blows and I didn't know if the suspect was bitten in the throat. I knew I would be sued again, and I was right.

As it turned out, the suspect's windpipe was crushed when John attempted the carotid restriction hold. The suspect was on parole for a pursuit he was involved in while driving a stolen car. The pursuit ended when a CHP officer crashed and was left a quadriplegic.

The suspect's family sued me and the department for a million dollars. After going through the depositions and talking with several city attorneys, the family settled for $50,000 dollars. I remember the incident every day when I look down at the long scars on my leg. Luke sure had a good bite.

Numerous officers later asked me, why did Luke bite my leg? I would explain that during the struggle both the suspect and I were rolling on the ground and the dog did not know who he was biting.

One day after I returned to work, I was driving down the street when I looked in my rearview mirror at Luke. The dog had a big smile on his face. I realized I was wrong about why Luke bit me.

The dog was not confused at all during the struggle and knew exactly who he was biting. That son of a bitch bit me on purpose. No pun intended.

Luke was paying me back for all the punishment he received during training. The bite was for using a shock collar on him, from time to time. It was for jerking on that damn leash so hard every night during training. Maybe dogs are smarter than we think. After that bite, I started being a little nicer to him during training.

## Chapter 41
## The Night I Killed a Guy

It is very seldom a cop comes across a burglary in progress at a commercial business. I was driving by an automotive store around four in the morning when I saw a burglar inside, going through the cash register.

I called for help and soon cops surrounded the business. There was a large fenced off yard, with several parked cars and other places to hide. The business and yard took up an entire city block.

I took my dog, Luke, and another K-9 handler, Dean, with me to search the business and yard. He was one of the few officers I could trust because we had been in so much stuff together in the K-9 unit.

We searched the inside of the business first. We found the broken window the bad guy entered, but no one was inside. The suspect must have gone into the yard while the perimeter was being established.

I began my area search with Luke and Dean as a cover officer. Soon Luke alerted to a large garbage dumpster. It was obvious the suspect was inside by the dog's body language.

It was really apparent when the dog jumped inside the dumpster on his own. We then heard the all too familiar screaming of someone being bitten.

I looked inside the dumpster and saw the suspect was holding a ten-inch screwdriver in his hand. Fearing he was going to stab the dog, I struck the suspect in the head with my baton.

It only took one good hit on the head to make him let go of the screwdriver. The bad thing about head wounds is they bleed profusely. We handcuffed the suspect and called for a code three ambulance for his head wound and dog bites. This guy was a crack head that weighed only 120 pounds.

There was a pool of blood on the ground where the suspect was sitting when the sector sergeant arrived. Any K-9 bite required the sector sergeant to complete a short use of force report.

I explained that I saw the suspect holding the screwdriver and attempted to strike him in the arm with my baton. He moved and was accidentally struck in the head.

Once the ambulance arrived, they took the suspect's vital signs and said he wasn't doing too well. They drove to the hospital code three, leaving Dean and I more than a little concerned about his condition.

A few minutes after the ambulance arrived at the emergency ward, a female officer who was at the hospital called our sector sergeant on the radio. She advised the sergeant that the guy who was just brought in by ambulance had died.

I felt sick to my stomach because I knew I didn't have to hit that guy to protect my dog. A dog's life shouldn't be worth as much as any human's, even if it is a police officer's partner.

K-9 officers become protective over their dogs, much like they would their own children. A special bound with a dog happens over time. They're more than a dog; they're our friend and partner.

A rush of panic overtook me. I may lose my job or worse yet, go to prison for excessive force. Dean pulled me to the side for a private conversation.

He also knew I didn't need to hit the guy and wanted no part of a death investigation. He told me he was going to say he was on the other side of the building when the suspect was hit.

After getting our stories straight, I looked at the sector sergeant who was taking a few notes, but didn't seem concerned about the incident. This scared me and I thought the homicide investigators would soon arrive with the internal affairs unit.

After a few more minutes, I couldn't take the sergeant's silence anymore. I then asked him about my suspect dying. The older sergeant looked at me like I was crazy and said, "What are you talking about?"

I told the sergeant that I heard on the radio my suspect, brought in by ambulance, had died. The old fart began to laugh his ass off. He told me that the guy who died was from the female officer's call. That guy died from an overdose.

The sergeant told me that my suspect only received a few stitches to the head and was fine. The old supervisor was pretty smart and asked me if there was anything wrong. I said everything was great now.

Dean didn't like the idea of doing anything shady. He knew I got a little violent during some arrests and didn't like to go with me on many calls after that incident.

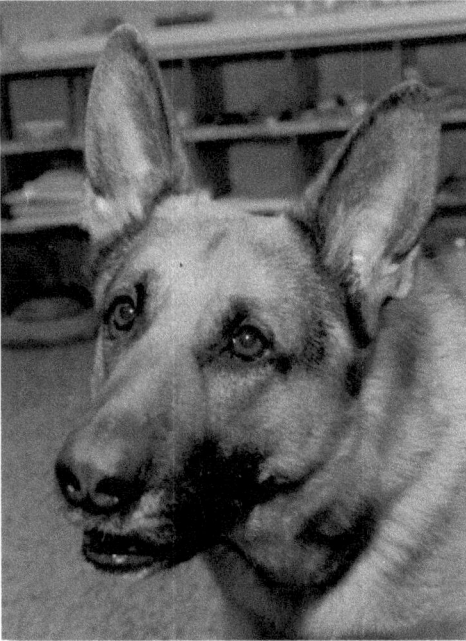

Buddy's head. He was a fierce dog who loved his job, but had a beautiful face.

## Chapter 42
## My Reputation

After being on the K-9 Unit for ten years, I earned the well-deserved reputation of being a hardworking, aggressive K-9 officer. The young rookie patrol sergeants were told to leave me alone by their patrol lieutenants.

Most of the swing shift and graveyard watch commanders were good friends of mine. We played on the same department football and softball teams, and had more than one beer together over the years.

The older supervisors knew I would listen to my personal "Bearcat 210" police scanner, which I mounted in my take-home K-9 unit. They knew I would be more than happy to handle all calls throughout the city that were best suited for a K-9 unit.

Back in those days, the police car radios did not have any scanning capability. Cops and dispatchers never knew what was happening in the next sector of the city. I frequently heard other police agencies on my scanner in vehicle pursuits coming into the city limits.

I would often advise our unaware dispatchers of the outside agency vehicle pursuit coming into the city. This was a big help for the dispatchers for the next several years until all police car radios had scanning capabilities.

Having a good reputation with the patrol sergeants and watch commanders gave me the opportunity to use my patrol dogs like I wanted to.

Because I didn't take advantage of my freedom, I didn't need any supervision. I am very proud to say I was a hard worker and was able to find and arrest a lot of really bad people in my career.

I did a lot of dirty jobs for the patrol sergeants, like crawling under homes with my dog looking for someone who just robbed a convenience store at three in the morning. Putting my dog in an attic or other hiding places were common things for me to do every night during various building searches.

At this stage in my K-9 career, I seldom, if ever, took any other officer with me during any of my searches. This raised eyebrows with many new patrol sergeants who demanded I take a cover officer for safety reasons.

I was always diplomatic with the young sergeants and would take a patrol officer along with me just to please them. After jumping over several backyard fences for the first two or three homes I searched, most of the patrol cops who were searching with me were glad to wait on a fixed perimeter location.

During most searches, I never knew if the suspect was armed with a gun, a knife, or any other potential weapon. The area or building to be searched was usually dark, giving the suspect the advantage of concealment.

It is hard to describe the mixture of fear and excitement while conducting a search late at night in some dark backyard with my dog. I always felt a little more pumped up when searching for a rape suspect or other vicious person who just hurt an innocent child.

The last thing I needed to think about during those arrests was having some cop as a potential witness in a use of force compliant. I wasn't shy about the amount of force I used during some arrests.

With today's modern equipment, I would not be able to work a police dog the same way. A police body camera would have prevented me from doing some of the things I shouldn't have done in the first place.

Today police officers have tasers to shock violent suspects into submission. Remote controlled flying drones, with night cameras that can see things in the dark, are now routinely used by the police.

The advance in technology in police work has made it much safer for the cop as well as the criminal. Nonlethal equipment such as tasers, pursuit spike strips, robots and drones give officers choices in dangerous situations, which they didn't have before. Cops now can use nonlethal options before firing their gun.

Sometimes in the heat of a violent struggle with a suspect, I would get scared and do some things that they didn't teach at the academy. Struggling on the ground with a suspect is one of the dangerous things a cop can do. An officer's handgun can be accidentally knocked out of the holster, or the suspect can rip it out with one big tug.

Most patrol officers wouldn't approve or understand the tactics I used that kept me alive during hundreds of late-night felony apprehensions. During many arrests I made while working a dog, I used speed, surprise, and violence of action to take the suspects into custody as quickly as possible.

If any suspect resisted or fought during apprehension, my dog and I always worked as a very effective team. After the suspects were handcuffed, I always made it a practice to talk to them. They were usually sitting in the rear of a squad car, waiting for an ambulance to arrive to treat their dog bites.

At first, these criminals were pissed off at me because they'd been bitten by my dog, but I knew how to talk to them. I used the same line when I talked with the older crooks who had been in prison at some point in their life.

I gave them respect and explained that they could have given up and surrendered when they knew my dog was searching for them. "It was nothing personal, but business is business," I'd tell them.

Showing concern for their dog bites and getting them medical treatment as soon as possible was the way I took care of things after an arrest with my dog. The way I talked with the parolees after their arrest and treated them with a little respect prevented many Internal Affair complaints. Parolees and hardcore criminals just want a little respect from cops, as strange as that may seem.

## Chapter 43
## Supervisors

I had many sergeants during my career. It was obvious which ones just wanted to climb the ladder and didn't care about anything else. As long as you did your job and didn't cause any problems, it didn't make any difference what sergeant you worked for.

It was amazing to see how many supervisors of all ranks tried to reinvent the wheel just to impress their bosses. They would talk on the radio just so their supervisor or lieutenant could hear them doing a good job.

Trying to impress others and make a name for yourself was how to get promoted. I was amazed at how some of my close friends changed once they were promoted in the ranks. People truly forget where they came from and the friends they worked with.

Good supervisors were rare. To find a sergeant who cared about the emotional health of officers after a horrible call, like a child's death, was unheard of. If an officer requested to go to counseling, they were seen as weak or crazy.

Police departments have come a long way in how they deal with the emotional aftermath officers go through after a critical incident. The sad fact is police offices are twice as likely to kill themselves than being killed at the hands of another person. Police work is not what you see on the on TV or the movies.

Many young supervisors are promoted very quickly and climb the chain of command. Unfortunately, some only spend a few years working on the streets and lack the experience of being a real cop.

Some egos got in the way of many major calls, which ended up in dumb school-kid arguments. The smart ones are promoted and then transferred to important areas such as planning or the property unit.

All departments need to be racially balanced and diversified to reflect the community's makeup. Some managers obviously are promoted due to their gender or race. Many supervisors are not the most qualified person as far as their experience and intelligence. This has always caused morale problems in any department.

During my thirty years, I became bitter at a lot of the managers in the department. There are few things more demoralizing than taking orders from an incompetent supervisor of any rank. The young supervisors would soon make daily decisions based on their vast street experience, which made the older cops want to puke.

It is extremely hard to listen to a young supervisor tell you how to search a building when you have done it a thousand more times than they have. It has always puzzled me why a manager with little street experience never utilizes an old cop's wisdom. Egos play a big part in a police department, just like anywhere else.

I worked around numerous front-line supervisors during my long career working the streets. Young sergeants with little street experience usually tried to over-supervise their officers to impress the watch commander.

I learned a lot of things from older patrol sergeants I worked around over the years. Two things the good supervisors did to take care of their officers after they were involved in a critical incident were to remove the officer from the scene as soon as possible, then notify the officer's family that he or she was safe.

Those same patrol sergeants also taught me that follow-up and encouragement are vital. They knew it was important for the officer to attend critical incident debriefing, then to seek a qualified mental health expert. The sergeants continued keeping the family up to date on the officer's status, and encouraged the officer's friends to stay in touch and listen.

Equally as important as what to do, are the things that the other officers and family members should not do. They shouldn't say everything will be fine. They shouldn't tell the officer that they know how it feels. Making promises and then not following up never helps, nor does giving too much advice.

Sixteen-inch hunting knife. The survival knife had a compass in the butt and a razor-sharp serrated blade. The suspect tried to stab Mike in the chest with the knife. Bear bit the guy's arm as he was swinging the blade. Bear may have saved Mike's life that night. Our dogs didn't get medals of valor, but Bear certainly deserved one for that arrest.

## Chapter 44
## Racial Profiling

I was a hardworking, aggressive cop with the reputation of being a little crazy. After I retired, I recognized my subconscious racial biases, which I am sure affected the way I treated people of color while I was a cop. No one likes to think bad things about themselves, and I am certainly no different. I have the humility to recognize that I did racially profile many people of color during my career.

Let me be clear. My entire career, I treated all people, "white, black or purple," the same way. I was always very nice to most people and gave everyone respect.

I often contacted different minorities in bad neighborhoods in order to find stolen cars or to make a felony arrest. Pulling over a car full of hardcore gang members was a common thing for me to do in the hood. I had a reputation of being a nice cop on the street. Smiling in public when driving by and giving people a little admiration goes a long way in the projects.

The gang members and crooks still knew not to run from me, because I didn't always play fair. I often got scared when arresting a violently resisting suspect and was not shy about how much force I used to make sure I didn't get hurt.

Being an aggressive young officer, I wanted to arrest as many people as I could for guns, drugs, and felony warrants. During my career, I arrested hundreds of felony suspects for various crimes after conducting legal traffic stops.

All cops know that in order for suspects to spend time in jail, the first requirement is for their successful prosecution in court. This means all evidence and statements must be obtained legally or they cannot be used. Any evidence or statements received as a result of illegally acquired evidence cannot be used. This is called fruit of the poisonous tree.

I am proud to say that during my career I never lied in any of my reports or when testifying in court. Putting a suspect in jail was not worth losing my job or going to jail for perjury. Plus, the rules of law were written for specific reasons that cops must respect and follow, even if they disagree with them.

Police officers also know that they need a thing called probable cause to conduct legal traffic stops and searches. They can't pull people over or stop them on the sidewalk if they didn't see them doing something wrong.

An officer must see a violation of the vehicle code or develop probable cause by having reasonable suspicion of illegal activity to make a legal stop.

Any cop knows it only takes a few blocks of following an average driver before they make a small violation of the vehicle code from not putting on their turn signal to not coming to a complete stop. Most people go over the speed limit.

I would always have legal probable cause or see a vehicle code violation before my stops. Many times, I pulled over a car occupied by several African Americans or Hispanics in a bad neighborhood, thinking they were gang members because of the clothes they were wearing. After stopping the car, it would only take a few seconds to see if the occupants were from a gang or were good kids.

I was never rude to anyone that I stopped. The young kids understood why I stopped them when I took the time and explained I was trying to make their community safe by getting guns off the street. I would always apologize and let them go as fast as possible.

Back then, black gang members either belonged to the Bloods, who wore red ball caps, or the Crips, who wore blue ball caps. The Bloods also wore red tennis shoes and long red bandannas, hanging out of their rear pants pocket like a flag. The Crips' color was blue.

Wearing your gang's colors was a big status symbol that was popular in the projects. You were expected to wear your gang's colors when you went outside. Sometimes it could get you killed.

Having the wrong-colored shoes on while walking in another gang's territory has gotten many innocent African Americans shot over the years. Top black prison gang members still have the influence to run their gang on the streets even from their cells.

White people have no idea what it's like to grow up in the projects and hear shots each night as they fall asleep. The white majority has always turned a blind eye to what takes place in bad neighborhoods and to people of color in our country, because it doesn't directly affect them.

Sometimes, the young minority occupants inside the car I stopped were innocent and had no criminal records. I didn't realize back then that the effects of being pulled over for no reason other than your skin color leaves a permanent memory in a young kid's mind.

I will always feel guilty for negatively affecting so many young people of color. In my quest to make a good arrest, I stopped many young innocent minorities in bad neighborhoods. Although I was always nice to them, they were all affected by the stop in some way.

My message to young officers is to think about how your contact may affect the minds of the innocent teenagers in the rear seat of the vehicle you stopped.

After being pulled over several times by the cops for doing nothing wrong, it is easy to see how people of color think police officers are racially biased towards minorities.

Most white kids cannot say they have been pulled over by the cops coming back from the show with a group of friends. Most kids of color have, which leaves a lasting lifelong impression.

## Chapter 45
## Rodney King

The camera does not lie. On March 3rd, 1991, a cell phone captured the Rodney King incident, which took place in Los Angeles, California. This single incident very possibly changed police work more than any other thing in history.

I have been involved in hundreds of use of force situations while arresting hardcore career criminals during my time in the K-9 Unit, and have never seen such an unwarranted and unjustified use of force in my career. The L.A.P.D. cops used obvious excessive force for that situation.

That one event, which showed police using unnecessary force, was so abusive in the minds of the public and police officials that it changed the way police were trained nation-wide.

Soon police officers in many departments throughout the country were wearing body cameras, which documented their every movement and contact. Cops now must report any type of abuse or misconduct they see committed by other cops on or off duty. If they don't do so, they risk losing their jobs, being sued, or even going to jail.

On rare occasions, as in the Rodney King case, officers may have to step in and take the appropriate immediate action during the actual acts of misconduct by any other fellow officers.

I could see the writing on the wall for me. It wouldn't be long before all the cops in my department would be wearing body cameras. This would mean every arrest I made in K-9 with my dog would have to be 100% by the book.

I soon realized you can't train old dogs to do new tricks. My days in the K-9 Unit were surely numbered if I had to wear a camera. It wouldn't have been very long before my violent instinctual techniques took over during a felony arrest, causing me to be fired, or end up in jail.

I look back at the hundreds of dog bites I witnessed and the numerous violent arrests I made in the K-9 unit and thank God that I am still alive and have a job. I knew it was time for me to move on. Working twenty years in the K-9 unit is a record in our department that won't be broken soon, if ever.

## Chapter 46
## Use of Force Report

If a suspect was injured during any arrest, a supervisor had to do a short use of force report to justify the officer's actions. This report was for liability and would be routed to the City's Risk Management Division for review.

Any K-9 bite would require the patrol sector sergeant to gather information to complete the report. Most sergeants had no problem writing the short report, which just contained the essential facts regarding the arrest.

Our department was separated into four sectors or areas where officers patrolled. Each sector had boundaries, with an area sergeant in charge. I loved being in K-9 because I could listen to my scanner and rove the entire city, picking out the best calls to go to.

My K-9 sergeant worked day shift, which was fine with me. I worked from seven at night until five in the morning and liked staying out of sight. Our shifts were ten hours a day, four days a week.

A few sergeants didn't like it when I went to any calls in their sector of responsibility. They all knew if I got a K-9 bite, they would have to do a damn use of force report. Some of our supervisors were so lazy they didn't like to make coffee, let alone write a short report.

Not that the sergeants didn't like me; however, they all knew I was an aggressive K-9 officer that got a lot of bites. I think they also knew I was a little crazy.

One early hot summer evening, I was called to a residence to help the patrol units. A wanted parolee, fresh out of prison, was inside and refusing to come out. The sector sergeant, Mark, was on the scene, along with four other officers.

The house was already surrounded by cops when I arrived. Mark was a friend of mine and had accompanied me on many searches. He gave me the green light to do my thing.

Mark and one other officer went with me into the residence. I trusted Mark because we had been through a lot of hot calls together. I didn't care that he was a supervisor. I knew he was tough and would back me up if things went bad.

I kicked the front door open and began a search, with Mark and the other officer following close behind. My dog alerted to a closed bedroom door. I kicked that door open and located the suspect, who briefly resisted.

A code three ambulance was requested because the suspect received several deep bites during the arrest. Mark and the other officers thanked me for my assistance, and I was off to the next call.

At the end of shift, Mark called me on the radio and asked me to meet him in the captain's office. When I arrived, he asked me to sit down. He then handed me his use of force report to review.

He was not laughing, and I was wondering if I may have gone a little overboard on this arrest. I will now show you Mark's exact use of force report, except for the suspect's name:

"On 7-13-99 I responded to 3201 64 Ave on a wanted subject refusing to come to the door. Officers had been dispatched to the location and were advised that a wanted parolee was inside.

The suspect, Paul Dodd, was listed by name, date of birth, and physical description. Records confirmed a felony want on Dodd. The complainant was a female who refused to give her name. K-9-4 Officer Garner responded to assist.

The owner of the house, Linda Service, arrived and advised no one should be in her home. Officers on scene had observed a male fitting Dodd's description look out the window and retreat to the rear of the house. Service gave me the key to her home and permission to search for the parolee or burglar.

Officer Garner made several loud admonishments at the front door, advising we were going to search with a police dog and anyone in the house would be bitten. After receiving no response, we entered the home.

At the east end of the hallway was a closed, locked door. Again Officer Garner made admonishments that we would be searching with a police dog and anyone hiding would get bit.

The suspect called out. 'I'm in here, I'm coming out, don't bite me.' Officer Garner kicked open the door and sent his K-9 into the darkened room. The K-9 bit the suspect, who was laying prone out on the floor. The suspect screamed, begging for the K-9 handler to stop the dog from biting him. Officer Garner kept yelling: that's what you get.

The dog continued to savage the unresisting suspect. The suspect continued to scream and beg the officer to stop the attack. The dog was now ripping flesh from several locations on the suspect. I became sickened by the spectacle and was momentarily shocked into inactivity by the sheer savagery of what I was witnessing.

I was galvanized into action when Officer Garner started to kick the prostate suspect over and over. I restrained Officer Garner and then turned my attention back to the suspect, who was sobbing incoherently.

I tried to pull the dog from the suspect, however this only resulted in greater tears to the suspect's flesh. The other officers and I threw a mattress over the K-9, walling him off from the suspect.

We were then able to drag the suspect out of the room and away from the vicious dog. This was the most vicious and unwarranted attack I have ever witnessed. I went to my car and cried. I have had nightmares ever since this barbaric travesty of justice.

Photographs of the interior door and suspect's ankle were taken by the crime scene investigator. All actions by the officers on scene were appropriate and within department policy."

Seeing all the major errors in Mark's report, I must have had a disturbed look on my face. Mark could not contain his laughter any longer. I then realized it was a joke. There were a few facts in the report's beginning that made me think it was real. It was the best use of force reports ever written, even if it wasn't true. Mark had a great personality and was liked by all.

## Chapter 47
## Get That Out Of My Locker

One slow, graveyard shift, a screaming voice no one could recognize came over the radio. "Code 900 officer down." The shot officer then gave his location, which was in the worst drug infested neighborhood in our city.

The officer attempted to pull his squad car up to a guy walking down the street to talk to him. Unknown to the cop, the man was a parolee who had just been shot in his side during a drug deal a few minutes earlier. The guy was higher than a kite on crack, which he had been smoking since he got out of prison a week earlier, and hadn't slept in days.

The sleepy cop stepped out of his car when the suspect turned and charged from only a few feet away. He started shooting, hitting the officer in the stomach just below his vest.

He fell to the ground and the bad guy took off running down the street. The officer was able to radio for help and give his location, but that was about it.

I was close by and the second officer to arrive on the scene. When I stepped out of my K-9 unit, I saw another cop holding the shot

officer's head in his lap. Up until that time, I
didn't know who it was.

Once I reached the two cops on the
ground, I saw it was my old partner and close
friend Sam who had been shot. Sam was my
friend who liked stopping bikes with his baton.

Sam didn't even notice me running up. I
then heard Sam say something to the other
officer that puzzled me for days. Sam told the
other cop to "get that shit out of his locker." I
had no idea what he was talking about, but
was very curious.

Dozens of cops responded and established
a large perimeter around several blocks. Four
K-9 units began searching for the armed
suspect. As luck would have it, my dog found
the guy hiding in a backyard.

Needless to say, I only used the minimal
amount of force, which was needed to take the
suspect into custody. He received numerous
dog bites and was admitted into the hospital for
other injuries sustained during the violent
struggle and arrest. I think his spleen had to be
removed.

Sam underwent surgery to get the two
bullets out of him and was in the hospital for
several weeks. I visited him a few days after
the shooting when he was still heavily
medicated. The first thing Sam did was to pull
back the sheets and show off his catheter.

After seeing that, I was not going to eat or have my code-7 soon.

I had to ask Sam what he was talking about when he told the other officer to get that shit out of his locker. Sam said he didn't know I had heard that comment, but trusted me and told me the story. He was afraid he was going to die and didn't want his wife getting some of his belongings from his locker.

Sam told me he took some Polaroid pictures of several female employees giving him a blow job in his uniform. The pictures were inside his locker, and he wanted them destroyed before his wife got his belongings.

Sam never fully recovered from being shot and had to retire a few years later. The cops that worked around him will always recall his wild antics and behavior. He was a rare type of cop that was a little crazy. That's why I liked him so much. I went to his funeral several years later and cried while remembering that night he was shot.

In the 1970s and 1980s, rampant sexism was an ugly aspect in law enforcement and every other profession in our country. Slowly, things changed away from the unwarranted pat on the bottom and other inappropriate language and behavior. Sexism in the workplace should not be tolerated in any way. This problem has improved over the years, but has regrettably not disappeared.

## Chapter 48
## Columbine School Shooting

I can remember seeing the breaking news of the Columbine shooting on TV on April 20th, 1999. The first arriving police officers heard gunshots from within the school and immediately called for the SWAT (Special Weapons and Tactics) team. Cops throughout the country were trained to freeze the scene and wait for SWAT in those situations.

Thirteen students were killed, and several others were injured before the SWAT team arrived. Back then, it was the common practice to establish a perimeter around a suspect shooting into a crowd of people and wait for SWAT.

As a result of the Columbine shooting, police tactics changed nationwide. Active Shooter tactics and training were soon taught to every cop in the country.

First responding patrol officers would still immediately call for a SWAT team to respond in emergency situations, but they would no longer wait for SWAT to arrive if a suspect was shooting at people.

If a suspect is actively shooting in any situation, cops are now trained to take immediate action. Waiting for SWAT while people are being shot is a thing of the past.

Cops now are trained to gather in a small group of patrol officers and go to the sounds of the gunfire in order to engage and stop the suspect as fast as possible.

Cops also receive specific training on how to use an emergency action team to quickly clear a room as they pass by while checking for additional suspects. These tactics and techniques have been adopted by most law enforcement agencies throughout the country.

## Chapter 49
## Saving a Life

One summer day, a fifty-five-year-old child molester, fresh out of prison, kidnapped an eight-year-old little Vietnamese girl. He pulled the girl off her bike in her own front yard, right in front of her terrified ten-year-old sister. The sick bastard threw her into his van and held her down as he sped away.

The sister gave us a great description of the suspect and vehicle, but she didn't get the license plate number. All the cops in the city were looking for the van. We all knew from experience it was a race against time before the little girl would likely be murdered after being sexually attacked.

An old homicide lieutenant spent five hours driving up and down every street around the victim's home looking for the van. He found the suspect's van only four blocks away, parked in the backyard of a house.

The vehicle's plate was run in the system and revealed the owner was a registered sex offender on parole for raping another small girl. Our lieutenant called for assistance.

The older sector sergeant responded, along with two other K-9 officers and Nick, a plainclothes detective. As luck would have it, I trusted the sergeant, who trained me when I was a rookie. The others who responded were not your typical cops. They were the best cops I had ever worked around.

We all knew we weren't going to play around with this asshole. These were exactly the kind of cops needed for this call. We all had been in several shootings each and had no problem with killing this son of a bitch.

A plan was quickly developed on how we were going to gain entry into the suspect's house. There was no time to wait for SWAT as we raced against the clock. The monster in the house was going to have to kill the girl because he knew he couldn't let her go free or he would be caught for sure.

We left one K-9 in the backyard after creating a diversion by breaking a front window out. When I tried to kick the front door open, we discovered the suspect had already pushed a heavy couch against it to slow the police down. After a few seconds, we gained entry into the living room and began searching the dark house.

The four of us entered a bedroom and saw a bed and nightstand. The bed was covered in blood, where the victim had been repeatedly raped for hours. A bloody rag and jar of Vaseline were on the nightstand. Only God knows what she had been through already. We just hoped to find her alive.

Nick then opened a closet door and all four of us got ready to shoot this sick son of a bitch. We knew the chances of finding the girl alive were slim to none, because he finished sexually torturing her.

Once the closet door swung open, we saw a tiny naked figure huddled in the corner. The poor girl had a gag in her mouth and her feet and hands were tied up with bailing wire.

I picked her up in my arms and ran outside, while the other officers continued to search the residence. The poor little girl was holding me around the neck as tight as she could when I knocked on a neighbor's door and asked them to watch her for a few minutes.

Looking back on things, I should have never done that. I should have given the victim comfort and held on to her until an ambulance arrived. The overwhelming feeling of wanting a piece of the suspect's ass made me run back across the street to his house. Once I stepped inside, I heard a loud struggle in the bathroom and ran to see if I could assist in the arrest.

The walls and floor were covered in the suspect's blood. The other officers had found him sitting on the toilet with a large knife lying next to him. He made the mistake of reaching for the knife.

The other officers, of course, used the minimal amount of force needed to affect an arrest, which sent him to the hospital for surgery.

The homicide lieutenant who found the car was waiting outside for us. After we made the arrest, he came inside the bathroom and saw all the blood. The lieutenant was from the old school and said, "I don't care if you shot this guy, just make sure you write a good report."

We all knew that he knew what had happened during the arrest. The suspect got life in prison with no chance of parole. The victim got life in her own prison of remembering the pain she endured, with little chance of forgetting that horrible day.

If you saw the look of horror on that naked little girl's face, tied up like an animal in a closet after being sexually tortured for hours, you might have a different view of the death penalty.

Years later, after my retirement, I had lunch with Nick and the other two K-9 officers that were on the call. We talked about the arrest and what each of us did. We all vividly remembered each detail, as if it had just happened.

All four of us agreed it was one of the best arrests we made in our careers, because we knew we saved the little girl's life that night.

## Chapter 50
## Another Routine Traffic Stop

One late night, I was paroling on the north side of town. This area was known for its high population of white trailer trash. During the dust bowl years, many Oklahomans migrated to our city, where they took up occupancy. My grandparents were among the people who moved here during that time.

The area was a known hangout for white prison gang members. In particular, the Aryan Brotherhood had high concentrations of members in that neighborhood. That prison group didn't like cops, and were known for their violent ways of life.

I saw a car driving with one brake light out. I drove alongside the car at a traffic light to see what the driver looked like so I could make an educated guess on whether or not I should stop him. If he was wearing a white collar, turned around backwards, and a robe, I probably wasn't going to stop him.

I didn't write traffic tickets, just stopped people in an effort to find guns, dope or a felony warrant. It was getting busy, so I would make this a fast stop just to run a warrant check on the driver, if he looked like a dirt bag.

Our department had classes about the public's negative perception of police profiling people at traffic stops. I can unequivocally say I have never known any cop to pull someone over solely because of their race.

It's not acceptable to stop a black family just because they are driving in a white neighborhood. However, seeing a young black man late at night driving slowly in a white neighborhood may make any cop suspicious regardless of their own race. Seeing a white guy driving around late at night in a black neighborhood would also be suspicious.

I looked over at the driver and saw the stereotypical prison tattoos covering his neck. I couldn't see the skin on his arms because of the ink from his numerous prison tattoos.

Some were works of art, but most were pictures of his gang crap. His large upper body and arms looked like he was a professional weightlifter, or fresh out of prison.

Figuring he may be a parolee at large, I planned to stop him at the next light. Once I activated my overhead lights, he pulled to the side of the road and exited his car. Assuming he might run, I stood up, removed my gun, and watched him walking back to me.

I kept my gun out, holding it down by my leg, when he approached my door. My police dog, Bear, was barking and growling at the guy through my open back window. Back in those days, we kept our rear windows all the way down in case we needed our dogs to jump out and help us.

Our dogs were highly trained not to bite from the car or jump out on their own. Today's K-9 units all have metal screens over the windows and the handlers have remote control door openers in case they need their dog.

This guy looked dangerous and was acting weird. He looked down at the gun in my hand and then did something that caught me off guard. This crazy bastard kissed my growling dog on the nose, saying "good doggie." He told me he loved dogs. This guy had no fear in him.

I kept my gun out and shoved him away, telling him to get back in his car, which he did. It was a miracle he wasn't bitten in the face. My dog bit several innocent people walking by my car even though he wasn't supposed to.

Still holding my gun by my side, I walked up to the driver and received his driver's license. I was not going to take a chance with this nut. A warrants and record check on him ran over my computer.

As I suspected, he had just been released from prison and was on active parole. However, he had no warrants and was not wanted. I later found out he was, in fact, a wanted parolee, but his felony warrant was not yet in the automated system.

I was going to call for another unit to assist me in searching his car when a vehicle pursuit close by came out over the radio. Officers were asking for a nearby K-9 unit, which was me, so I gave his license back and headed for the pursuit.

I didn't realize I almost died that night until the next day. The driver of the car I stopped was a top enforcer of the Aryan Brotherhood. An enforcer is a title that a person receives in prison. They have to earn the title once they have committed numerous assaults or murders on the orders from others in the gang.

This guy had been planning to break a fellow gang member out of our county jail for several months. They were waiting for the right time when the inmate would be transported to a dentist appointment. The breakout was planned for the following day.

The dentist's office was not in the jail's building. Prisoners would have to be transported in a small secure jail van to the dentist's office downtown. The appointment was at three o'clock the next day.

Both subjects had been communicating with each other through other people. Somehow, they found out there would only be one deputy present during the prisoner transport to the dentist appointment.

This was the time they were waiting for. Once the lone deputy exited the jail van at the dentist's office, he started to open up the sliding security door. The guy I had stopped the night before was waiting in some bushes with a gun.

The deputy didn't have a chance. He was shot in the head and fell to the pavement in the busy office complex. The suspect then walked over to the deputy and shot him once more in the head, just for extra measures.

The van's security door had not been opened yet, and the guy didn't know what to do. He used a bar to partially pry open the door, then peeled the door back with his bare hands. In doing so, he injured his arm when it got pinned and crushed.

The two made their escape in the same car I had stopped the night before. The car was found abandoned a short time later in that same neighborhood. The two left town soon after they broke free.

The deputy didn't die; however, he was blinded. His life would never be the same because of some crazy asshole. I felt horrible for not searching the car the night before. Maybe I could have prevented this incident.

Then I thought back to how the driver walked back to me. I have wondered if he was planning to shoot me until he saw my gun out. I never patted him down, so it was unknown if he had a gun on him while at my door. One thing is for certain. This guy was a cold-blooded killer who would not have thought twice about shooting me if he could have.

Both suspects were on the run for over a week. Intelligence reports indicated even other Aryan Brotherhood safe houses didn't want these guys around because of the intensive manhunt for them.

Both of them were eventually arrested. The guy I stopped had been injecting heroin into the infected arm he had injured during the jail escape. He was later found hiding under a house.

## Chapter 51
## Rogue Humor

Some cops have a sick sense of humor. They laugh at the horrible things they see on calls, as if they were not real. The public would be shocked at some of the inappropriate comments made by cops at the most gruesome crime scenes.

This response is a protection mechanism many cops use in order to deal or cope with some negative thing they experience. Making a joke and laughing at a crime scene is a lot more acceptable than breaking down in tears and vomiting. I have seen young cops with a dazed look on their faces after seeing a decomposed body for the first time. People handle stress in many different ways.

I had a reputation for saying terrible things at the strangest times. Even the veteran cops would look at me and walk away, shaking their heads at how crazy I was.

The things I saw bothered me at times. However, I thought it was important to say something funny in order to break the tension of the investigation we had to do.

One night, a female pedestrian was struck by a train as she walked across the tracks downtown. A lot of cops have a morbid curiosity, and I was no different. I responded to the scene, only to find four other cops looking down at the dead body.

The girl's body was not in that bad of shape, as compared to some train versus pedestrian accident victims I had seen over the years. Her torso was on one side of the tracks and her severed arm was only a few feet away on the other side of the tracks.

The arm was cut off just above the elbow. It was a creepy thing to see because there was not an ounce of blood on the arm. The train's wheel must have pinched all the arteries and veins closed. The arm looked like it belonged to a store mannequin.

As we all were looking down at the bizarre spectacle, I couldn't resist any longer. I told the other officers that "we should at least give the girl a hand." They all moaned at my stupid comment and walked away. My rogue humor continued with me my entire career, which helped me through some rough calls.

I became addicted to the nightly adrenalin rushes I received while being on so many exciting calls. Conducting K-9 searches for people with guns was a common occurrence in the K-9 unit.

The more dangerous the search, the more fun it was to me. The chances I took slowly got out of hand over the years. Going to the hospital emergency room six times for various injuries did not slow me down. Stitches and concussions were minor compared to the price some cops had to pay. Getting hurt was a scary reality that I tried not to worry about.

Today police supervisors or patrol sergeants must be conscious of the ugly horrible things their officers see and experience in order for them to be aware of potential problems which may occur down the road. Signs and symptoms of PTSD may not show up for weeks, months, or even years after the incident or bad call.

Critical Incident Debriefings are now commonplace in many departments nationwide after the death of an officer or a life-threatening event takes place.

## Chapter 52
## I Didn't Try To Run Him Over

One winter, the city was plagued with a series of armed robberies at pizza restaurants. A crew of three armed, masked gunmen robbed over twenty pizza parlors within a month. The suspects always wore the same ski masks and clothes, and carried out each robbery in the same fashion: fast. Two suspects would watch the doors and rob the customers, while the other guy would force the manager to open the safe.

Several shots were fired during the last few robberies, which meant the suspects were becoming more bold and violent. They punched and kicked people during each robbery, to get their point across, that "they weren't fucking around."

On one occasion, a victim thought one guy had an Uzi under his coat. This time, one of the suspects shot the manager in the leg because he was moving too slow.

A witness saw the suspect vehicle leave the scene. Our dispatcher gave out a good description of an old brown Ford Maverick with a partial license plate that started with ARS.

I knew I should start towards the drug hangouts to look for the suspect vehicle. They were surely crackheads that needed some dope. When a group of guys rob that many restaurants in that short of time, several things are certain: the robberies will get in their blood for the fun and easy money (they do it for the excitement and drug money), and at least one suspect will be just out of prison.

Ten minutes after the robbery call went out, I drove by a small store in a bad part of town. This store gave out free coffee to the cops, so they wouldn't keep getting robbed. As I drove by, I saw a marked squad car in the parking lot. One of our old-time cops was drinking coffee inside the store, while talking to the clerk.

I then saw a brown Ford Maverick with the same partial plate park next to the squad car. Three young men wearing puffy jackets exited the car. They were laughing their asses off while walking inside the store. There was no doubt these were the robbery suspects. And they were all probably armed with guns.

I could not contact the old cop in the store by radio because the three suspects might hear the conversation. I sat in my K-9 car across the street until the three hoods exited the store. Once they were outside, I radioed for help and followed the suspect's car when it pulled out of the parking lot.

It only took half a block before the suspects realized I was following them, and the pursuit was on. The suspect vehicle turned down a gravel alley and tried to speed away.

I couldn't see where I was driving for a few seconds because the flying dust was blinding me, but these guys had to be stopped at all costs. It was only a matter of time before they were going to kill someone during one of their robberies.

The vehicle turned down several streets and the rear door opened up several times. It was obvious the rear passenger was getting ready to jump out of the moving car and try to run away on foot. This was a common technique that I had seen many times before.

The car was going about thirty miles per hour and made a right turn when the guy in the rear seat jumped out. An armed suspect was tumbling on the ground when I ran him over, with the front and rear tires of my K-9 vehicle. I felt my car tires rolling over his body and knew this guy was dead.

The suspect vehicle continued to drive away at a high speed, with several other units in pursuit. I jumped out of my police car expecting to find the mangled, dead body of the guy I just accidentally ran over.

To my amazement, the suspect jumped to his feet and ran down an alley with a handgun in his hand. I started chasing the guy on foot with my dog when the asshole made his second mistake. The guy turned and pointed a gun at me, and that's all it took.

I shot at the guy four times, hitting him twice in the upper body. He jumped a fence, and a perimeter of cops surrounded the block. I then started to search each backyard for the suspect with my police dog.

I wondered how I was going to write my report. How was it going to look that I just ran over the guy with my car and shot him twice? The suspect now was going to likely get bitten by my police dog, if he was found hiding. I had never heard of any suspect ever being run over by a police car, shot twice and then bitten by a K-9, all in one incident.

As luck would have it, the suspect was found hiding under a bed, after he changed clothes and put on a woman's wig. The suspect did something else that was very smart. He wrapped two tennis shoes around his right forearm with a tee shirt and towel.

The suspect had the presence of mind to make a homemade K-9 sleeve for protection from a police dog's bite in case he was found hiding. He changed his clothes and put on a wig, all after being shot twice.

The extra padding from the shoes on each side of his arm made excellent protection from the police dog. I had never encountered a suspect using shoes wrapped around their arm for protection after arresting hundreds of people with my police dogs.

The suspect had not been bitten when found, but he was bleeding to death from the gunshot wounds to his torso. It was lucky he was found when he was, because he needed immediate surgery to stop the internal bleeding. One bullet was left inside him because it was too close to a vital organ to be removed.

The suspect vehicle was stopped and the bad guys, who were fresh out of prison, were arrested. The guys each got around eight years in prison. Any experienced cop will tell you how dumb some crooks are. It is unreal how many crooks will get out of prison and start committing the exact same types of crimes that sent them to the joint years earlier.

Each of our pizza suspects got out of prison around the same time, years later. It didn't take long before the city was having a rash of "take over" robberies of pizza joints. We were having two robberies each night for several weeks by three masked men, all armed with guns.

The robbery detectives did their job, and the same suspects were all soon picked up for multiple robberies and parole violation. This time they got a lot more time than eight years in prison to think about their next crime wave.

I was later asked by a close friend in the K-9 unit if I ran the suspect over on purpose. No, it was an accident, is what I told him. Cops are not trained to use a vehicle as deadly force.

Later in my career I accidentally hit several more fleeing suspects with my car. The bad guys were armed with guns and were running down the street. On both occasions, I was driving close behind them when they tried to cut in front of me. One guy was wanted for carjacking an old lady, and the other suspect was wanted for a business burglary.

These two guys were luckier than the first suspect. He sustained broken bones, internal injuries and two gunshots, after being run over. Both of the last two guys just bounced off my police car's windshield and received a lot of bruises.

I was very lucky when I hit the three suspects with my car when they were running away, because they all had guns. It would have been a hell of a lot more dangerous for me if I had to conduct an area search, with my police dog in some dark backyard, for an armed suspect. A guy running, armed with a gun, is bad news for the public as well as the police.

In my career, I knew seventeen cops in the department that had been shot on duty. Some were very close friends. I planned on not being the next. A cop has to do what they have to do to stay alive. It's better to be judged by twelve than carried by six.

My three encounters with the gunmen were during life and death situations. If my police car had a dashboard camera which captured the incidents, I might have lost my job.

In today's world, even with an officer's life in extreme danger, any injury of an armed suspect by an officer will be reviewed and criticized by their department as well as the public. Unfortunately, cameras don't always portray the best picture of what really happened. Many variables at a scene that cameras can't possibly capture on film must be taken into account.

## Chapter 53
## Look I Can Fly

One late night, a suspect broke into a Radio Shack Store inside a large shopping mall. A patrol officer saw the suspect inside the mall and requested a K-9 unit. While I was responding with my dog, the suspect fled out a rear door into the neighborhood.

When I arrived to do an area search, I observed the police helicopter over my head. The chopper was circling the area, searching the backyards with its bright spotlight. The mall was next to a four-lane street, which didn't have much traffic on it that late at night.

My dog stayed in the car while I walked across the street to talk to the officer who last saw the suspect. I usually started my K-9 searches exactly where the suspect was last seen. I always liked to talk to the cop to get the suspect's direction of travel and good description.

People would be amazed at the unusual places suspects hide from the police. Many times, they hide only a very short distance from where they were last seen.

After talking with the officer, I walked back across the street to get my dog out of the car. I was looking up at the helicopter while talking to the copilot on my hand-held radio.

Out of the corner of my eye, I saw a white flash coming at me from my right side. It was a small Porsche race car coming directly at me. The young male driver was also looking up at the helicopter and never saw me walking out in front of his car.

I tried my best to jump over the top of the low-profile car. My feet hit the hood just above the headlights, spinning my body sideways into the windshield. I bounced off the windshield like a ping-pong ball and flew up into the air as the car traveled beneath me.

Traffic investigators later determined I flew forty-five feet in the air, landing on the sidewalk. The car was going 35 MPH at impact. No brake marks were found. While I was flying in the air, a strange but vivid thought went through my mind. For a split second, I thought I saw another cop getting hit by the car. It was a complete out-of-body experience. I knew for sure it was someone else getting hit by the car.

The thought was so short-lived that I was still flying in the air when I realized it was me that had been struck by the car. Once my twisting body hit the sidewalk with a dull thump, I thought I may die from my injuries. The next few seconds were a blur of activity.

Several cops who saw the accident later told me they thought I was dead after I got hit so hard. The cops ran up, telling me not to move, and that an ambulance was on its way. One cop requested a hospital life flight helicopter, which scared the hell out of me. I was feeling no pain at all and wondered what injuries they saw.

Were broken bones sticking out somewhere? I couldn't take not knowing what my injuries were, so I stood up to look at myself.

The other officers protested, yelling at me to lie down because I was in shock. I took off my shirt and bullet-proof vest and saw no obvious injuries. I was feeling pretty lucky when the rush of pain hit me in the legs and made me collapse.

The ambulance arrived, and I made another trip to the emergency ward. This was my fifth time being taken to the hospital, in a code three ambulance, for injuries I got on the job. I wasn't accident prone, just an aggressive officer who got involved in a lot of dangerous calls.

I was extremely lucky that my fat head didn't hit anything during the accident, and there were no broken bones or internal injuries. When I woke up the next morning, both my legs were a dark blue color from the ankles to the hip. Getting out of bed was impossible because of the pain. I had to pee into a Gatorade bottle for the next week.

The physical injuries went away with time. However, the fear of cars remained inside my head for years. Being around a lot of traffic always scared the hell out of me after that call. I stopped doing routine traffic stops on busy streets or freeways.

Off duty, I would never walk in front of a slow-moving car in a store parking lot, even if the driver waved me across. I once told a counselor that I was glad I was so paranoid about cars. I knew, because of that bad experience, my caution would prevent me from getting hit by a car again.

The driver of the car received a citation for not yielding the right of way for a pedestrian. I felt bad for the young man because the accident was just as much my fault as his.

Several years later, I encountered the same driver while I was having my dinner, or Code-7, at a Chinese restaurant. He was sitting at a table next to me and asked if I was the K-9 cop that was hit by a car crossing a street.

He was a very nice kid and explained that he was the driver of the car and wanted to apologize to me for almost killing me that night. The young guy explained he still experienced constant flash backs of the incident. He told me he dreamed of me bouncing off his windshield, then flying through the air like a rag doll.

I told the poor guy that he shouldn't feel bad because I was not looking where I was going when I crossed the street. He thanked me, shook my hand, and said he was glad I wasn't seriously hurt.

I had never thought about how the driver of the car felt after hitting me. After that close call with death, I thought about everyone's feelings while at work. I started thinking about how dangerous my job was and how lucky I was to be alive. There were so many close calls with death and serious injury over the years, I began worrying about getting hurt for the first time in my career.

## Chapter 54
## The Blue Stigma

The negative stigma of asking for help with my mental health stopped me from getting the help I needed. This caused several difficulties during my career.

At times, the images and flashbacks of the horrible events I experienced were so disturbing I thought about taking my own life to escape my deep emotional pain.

The constant replaying of the same movie and experiencing all the emotions that were originally felt, just as if the incident had just occurred, was a secret problem I had.

The stigma of other cops thinking I was crazy, or a 5150, stopped me from getting the help I needed. I made several common excuses and never tried to get assistance for a problem I tried to deny I had.

I thought I would get better on my own after time, which turned out to be a joke. Thinking other cops wouldn't want to work around me if they thought I was unstable was one of my reasons for not seeking help. The fear of job ramifications also stopped me. I was worried about my future chances of promotion or transferring to another unit.

Today's officers have regular training on the importance of mental health. They are encouraged to seek help from confidential specialists who have their offices located away from the police department.

Trained experts now guide officers through group after-action debriefings following critical incidents. This is now commonplace in most agencies.

## Chapter 55
## Search to the Death

When a police officer is shot on duty, all hell breaks loose until the suspect is arrested. Numerous police cars respond from every agency, with sirens blaring and lights flashing. Being in the K-9 unit for such a long time, I searched for a dozen suspects who had shot at various cops on different occasions.

Bill was a top-notch cop who worked with a great partner, Dave. They worked as a team, looking for felony suspects in the bad part of town. Almost every night, they would chase down some wanted guy or get into a vehicle pursuit. They were two of the best cops in our department.

Bill was a very talented young man, who everyone liked. The girls liked him because he was so good looking, while the guys admired him because he was a stud. He played college football and was our department's star softball player.

They conducted a traffic stop on a parolee who had a felony warrant for his arrest. The car sped up, then slowed down, as if the suspect was going to bail out on foot and run.

Dave and Bill were faster than most cops, and this guy wasn't going to run very far. Once the car stopped, the driver's door flung open, so Bill and Dave ran towards the car. During their careers, they had chased so many bad guys who ran from cars that this was routine for them.

As Bill ran to the passenger side of the suspect's vehicle, the parolee had not exited yet. Just as Bill reached the car, he was shot in his upper body. Bill yelled out, "Oh God" and fell into the street. The bullet just missed his vest and hit him in the armpit area.

Dave ran after the fleeing driver and exchanged several shots with him in a dark field. The guy jumped over a fence and Dave radioed for help. Dozens of patrol cars were now responding from all over the city. Dave ran back to his best friend and partner. He then called for a hospital helicopter because Bill's condition was bad.

Another good friend on the K-9 unit, Ron, and I arrived at the scene about the same time. The SWAT team was on their way. We were told we couldn't start our search until the SWAT team showed up.

That pissed us off because we were losing valuable time, which might allow the suspect to escape. We also wanted to find him without a lot of SWAT officers as witnesses.

A several block perimeter had been established, with a lot of help from outside agencies. When a cop is shot, the bond of the badge is very apparent among all officers. There is no distinction between agencies, just a mutual feeling of wanting to get that son-of-a-bitch who shot a fellow cop.

Once the SWAT team arrived, three teams were formed and a slow, methodical backyard search was started. Ron and I did not like searching with the SWAT teams because we couldn't search the way we normally did.

They wanted us to do a meticulous search of every backyard. Our dogs could usually find a suspect in a short time, however, working with SWAT took hours.

We had to do what the SWAT team wanted. Ron and I had conducted thousands of area searches. We hated to listen to officers ask us every few seconds if our dog was picking up anything. They were in charge, and we had to do it their way.

A detective, who just came back from the hospital, drove up to the search area while Ron and I were talking to each other. The detective then told both of us that Bill had just died.

Until this point, both Ron and I had no idea Bill had been injured so critically. We thought he was hit in the vest and was just going to have blunt force trauma injuries.

Ron and I were stunned. We couldn't talk for a few seconds while we took in the complete surprise and shock of his death. We walked to a dark private area before continuing our search with the SWAT team.

Both of us also liked Bill very much because he was such a nice guy. We agreed that if we found the suspect, we were going to kill him. Of course, we were going to use the minimal amount of force necessary to affect the arrest of this cop killer. We were going to shoot him only if we had to, in order to prevent further injury to other officers. Want to buy a bridge?

The suspect was found several hours later during the search. Another K-9's team dog found the suspect's hat under a truck, in a rear yard. A SWAT sergeant saw the guy hiding behind an old refrigerator, with the gun still in his hand. The piece of shit was told to drop the gun, which he did. It was later found his gun had jammed and he could not keep firing it.

The SWAT team then leaned the suspect over the refrigerator to handcuff him. I was not searching with my dog in that backyard. I was with the other K-9 unit and SWAT team during the find and arrest.

Once the suspect was handcuffed, he was leaned over a washing machine to be further searched. I was only a few feet away when the rage in me took control for a split second. I took one step towards him, ready to kick him in the face as hard as I could.

Luckily, I stopped myself and no one else saw what I almost did. If I had kicked the suspect, I would have been fired, criminally prosecuted for civil rights violations, and sued in civil court.

That was one of many reasons I didn't like bringing other officers with me during searches. I couldn't do some things I would have liked to, over the years, because of too many witnesses.

The suspect got life without the possibility of parole. Dave got life remembering his best friend being shot and killed in front of him. Thinking of Dave hearing Bill crying out for God in his last few seconds of life is something that always brings tears to my eyes. Dave went through great personal loss earlier in his career and I wondered how much could one person take.

Dave's girlfriend, Emily, had also been an officer in our department. She could have been a model if she wanted because she was so beautiful. The year before Bill was killed, Emily was working on the graveyard shift. Another officer was chasing a stolen car, so Emily drove towards the pursuit. A drunk driver pulled out in front of her as she rounded a turn on the road.

Emily swerved to avoid a collision and struck a wall to a business at high speed. Dave was working that night and heard the unusual sounding voices of the officers on the radio. He knew an officer had just been hurt in an accident, but he didn't know who it was or their condition.

Dave then heard them ask for a life flight helicopter, which could only mean the injuries were bad. Another officer told Dave it was his girlfriend that was in the crash. He raced to the hospital. However, it was too late. Emily had died from massive internal injuries.

Emily was more than well liked in our department. She was loved by many. Emily had a way of bringing a smile to someone's face, even if she had just arrested them. She truly was a lady who always treated people with respect and dignity.

In a space of a little over a year, Dave lost his girlfriend and partner in two separate incidents while on duty. Somehow, he kept his sanity and continued to do a great job in the department.

Dave had been in several shoot-outs and received many awards and medals of valor. He went on to be promoted to sergeant, but he never forgot his love for Emily or the good times chasing bad guys with Bill.

It was scary for me to think about killing the suspect when I found him. I am glad I never found out if I could have shot the suspect during that moment of anger. Taking a human life is a sickening thing under any circumstance.

Back in those days, cameras were not a part of police work yet. There were no dashboard cameras in patrol cars and cops didn't wear body cameras.

If cameras were a part of police work back then, Ron and I would not have talked about killing the suspect. I wouldn't have thought about kicking him in the face or doing anything else wrong. Cameras have kept many officers in line and stopped them from getting in trouble and doing something they would later regret.

## Chapter 56
## Another Friend Shot

One spring evening, two close friends of mine were looking for a felony suspect in a low-income housing complex. These two cops, George and Dave, worked as a team for ten years and were legends in our department. They once made more felony arrests in one month than the entire graveyard unit did.

Their supervisors gave them the freedom to do what they wanted, something seldom given to other officers. They didn't handle family fights or car accidents. These guys just looked for the real bad guys and almost always found them.

They spotted their wanted crook on a bicycle and ran after him on foot. The suspect drove his bike around a corner of a building, jumped off it, and ran away on foot. George used his imagination and jumped on the bad guy's bike, and pedaled after him. Dave was a lot older and was not as fast as George and the suspect.

George rode the bike around a corner, only to find the suspect hiding with his gun out. The suspect ambushed George as he rounded the corner and shot him twice. George sustained two life-threatening wounds, which kept him off work for over a year. He almost died that day.

Dave found his partner, who he loved like a brother, lying in a pool of blood. The entire complex was closed off with dozens of cops from different agencies, and several other K-9 units began the search for the armed suspect.

I knew if I found the suspect and he made a fast movement, I may have to shoot him. I also knew it was hard not to move when being bitten by a police dog.

The feeling of using a police dog to find someone you were likely going to kill is something you don't forget. The adrenalin rush of knowing you could be shot was now at a different level than the normal K-9 search. I liked the feeling, and would try to experience it as much as I could for the rest of my career. It was simple: I may kill him, or he may kill me.

Another K-9 officer's dog found the suspect hiding inside a duplex an hour after the shooting. The housing complex contained several hundred duplexes and many places to hide. This was one of the best finds I had ever seen by any police dog. I was jealous it wasn't my dog that made the find.

The other K-9 alerted to the outside of a duplex, located half a mile away from where the suspect was last seen running, an hour earlier. He was ordered outside and was arrested without further incident. The suspect's gun was found hidden in a garbage bag in the kitchen.

An untrue, vicious rumor started a day after the arrest. The suspect made a complaint that a cop sat in the back seat of the patrol car he was in after his arrest. He said the officer asked him if he liked to shoot cops, and then squeezed his nuts as hard as he could.

Some officers thought I was the one who did it. I told them I would never do such a cowardly thing to a handcuffed prisoner who had just ambushed a good friend.

My last year in K-9, I stopped wearing my bullet-proof vest because it was more exciting to go on hot calls without it. In my mixed-up mind, I had to be a better cop and be more careful if I didn't wear my vest. There was no second chance.

I still used good officer safety techniques and was cautious on calls. I just got a little extra adrenalin high from not wearing my vest. It was much like a heroin addict who needs more and more dope each time to reach their needed high. I needed to go to the most dangerous calls to reach my adrenalin high.

## Chapter 57
## Hypervigilance

I will now try to explain *hypervigilance*. Cops experience things each shift that make them think of their own personal safety. Cops work alone and often think of the worst scenarios in order to stay alive. Let me give you an example.

When an officer conducts a traffic stop, he is always watching the driver's hands as he approaches the car. If the driver drops his wallet and starts reaching around on the floorboard for it, the officer may think he is retrieving a gun. A rush of adrenalin and fear will hit the officer until the danger is no longer apparent.

Cops have to be suspicious in order to stay alive. Officers often think about how they would react if confronted with a gunman or other types of emergencies. Cops must always expect the unexpected on every call. Watching a person's hands when making contact with anyone was second nature at all stops.

Being in the K-9 unit, I went from one hot call to another all night long. I never had the chance to come down from the adrenalin high from my last call. This pumped-up feeling stayed with me all night. It seemed I never took a deep breath or relaxed during my shift.

I was lucky many times during my twenty years working in the K-9 Unit. It's a funny thing, but I didn't feel lucky back then. Being young and inexperienced made me very naïve about my own mortality.

I never worried about the dangers of the job. The dangerous part of the job is what made it so much fun. Looking back on my career, it's amazing I wasn't shot, stabbed, or killed in a pursuit. I made a lot of dumb mistakes that could have easily gotten me hurt.

I was an extremely aggressive K-9 handler who loved working my police dogs to search for felony suspects each night. Using a police dog to search for a criminal who is hiding is one of the most dangerous things a cop can do.

Working in a police K-9 unit for two decades is virtually unheard of in any police department in the country because of the inherent hazards of handling so many high-risk calls for so long.

The critical balance between job and family is an important aspect of this book. Liking the job too much and spending too many hours at work had a dramatic consequence on my whole family.

I found many guns in cars after pulling some shady looking character over. Nothing gets a cop's attention more than finding a hidden gun during a pat down search on a person.

I can still vividly recall the excitement I felt when I pulled over a Hell's Angel on his motorcycle one night. They had a large club house nearby, and I was afraid his friends would soon drive by. The big ass dude was proudly wearing his colors or vest, with the Hells Angels name on it.

He didn't expect me to pat him down for a minor traffic offense. The asshole started to say I was harassing him, which I was, because he was a biker. I immediately called for a backup unit. I then made the mistake of patting the guy down for weapons before my back-up unit arrived to assist me.

As soon as I reached in his coat, I felt a small 25 caliber handgun. As I tried to pull the gun out of his pocket, he pinned my arm against his body. The big ass biker then let my arm loose, when he felt the barrel of my gun poking the back side of his head.

One more second of him struggling for his gun and I was just about to shoot him in the back of his head. I handcuffed him without any further problem and learned not to like bikers.

Patrol cops have time to come down from the adrenalin high of an exciting call during their shift. Writing reports and doing other paperwork takes up a lot of a patrol officer's time. K-9 officers were spoiled and rarely took any reports. This was to keep us available for pursuits and high priority calls throughout the city.

I soon became addicted to an adrenalin high, because I loved the excitement of all the dangerous calls I went on each night. My body would physically change during these events. Every one of my senses became more acute. I felt more alert when I was in this state of mind.

The feeling was euphoric, and I couldn't get enough of it. It was exactly like a drug addict, needing his daily fix. It was necessary to stay in the hyper-vigilant state of mind throughout my shift in order to stay alive on all the hot calls. I didn't mind staying busy during my shift because I enjoyed feeling alive and full of energy after a vehicle pursuit or finding a suspect with my dog.

Now I understand why people undertake risky behavior, such as skydiving or mountain climbing. The calculated brush with death is strangely an enjoyable experience.

During my shift, I often would go on numerous high-risk calls that kept me on an adrenalin high all night long. I would be so amped up throughout my shift it was impossible to go to sleep when I got home.

On my days off, I went through adrenalin withdrawals. I couldn't wait to get back to work to get my next fix. I only slept five hours a night before waking, then couldn't go back to sleep.

My wife woke up every night because I'd grind my teeth when I slept. I often had scary dreams about the job where my gun wouldn't fire during a shootout. My dreams got worse as the years passed by. I would wake up screaming, scaring my wife.

Most civilians only experience these intense emotions a few times in their lives. A car crash or other close calls with death are fortunately a rare occurrence for most of the public. There are a lot of dangerous professions. However, the daily risks are known to the employees.

It's the unknown dangers or hazards in police work that are different from most other jobs. Cops have no control over what bizarre calls they get sent to. As I got older, I knew life was getting shorter and the close calls were starting to take their toll on me. My mortality was always on my mind, even off duty.

I knew something was wrong with me when I almost punched a seventy-year-old lady in the supermarket. The produce spray system periodically made a ringing sound before the water was sprayed on the vegetables. The system rang out, and scared the hell out of me one day when I was shopping. I spun around with clenched fists, scaring the poor lady standing behind me to death. She apologized and quickly walked away.

On another occasion, a kid on a skateboard came up behind me really quick and scared me. I jumped back and started to swing at him, almost striking him out of a fear reaction.

This reaction to loud noises and quick movements is called an exaggerated startle reflex. I get startled very easy. I still get scared a few times a week from some innocent noise or movement. This affliction will likely not go away for the rest of my life.

The sensation of being pumped up all night after going on so many hot calls for so many years took its toll on me in many different ways. I have nightly dreams about the job even after being retired for several years.

I wasn't the only cop who loved their job. There were other cops who went the extra mile to make good arrests and track down wanted criminals. Most cops, however, just handled the calls in their district and wrote a few tickets.

Only a few patrol officers had the reputation of being hunters. These were the best cops in the department. They weren't told by supervisors to look for bad guys. They took it upon themselves to look for wanted suspects between their radio calls. On some occasions, they used their own time to look for the bad guys who hurt innocent children.

Unfortunately, the best officers in the department are at the highest risk of suffering the negative effects of hypervigilance. The love of the job is often the cause of many family problems.

When I got married at the age of twenty-one, I believed that I would be with my wife, Lori, for the rest of my life. She was truly my first love, and I loved her with all my heart. When I got the news about being hired as a police officer, I promised her I'd quit if the job ever changed me in ways she didn't like. I explained that I could always get another job, but there was only one Lori for me.

I loved my family very much. My problem was I was always thinking about the job instead of them. I was a great cop who made a lot of arrests. Unfortunately, I can't say the same about being a good father.

I thought that working weekly over-time jobs and making a lot of money would be the right thing to do for my family. Deep down inside, I knew they needed my time rather than my money.

On my days off, I sat around watching TV and drinking beer. I was usually bored stiff and wished I was at work. When I went on bike rides with my family, I drove them nuts by being overly protective. I would constantly tell them to not ride in the streets and watch out for cars. It got to the point where I was no fun to be around.

After a twenty-nine-year marriage, my wife divorced me after my third heart surgery. She got half my retirement and our house. I was devastated and gave her everything she wanted. I can't blame her for liking a good looking twenty-year-old kid.

Our arguments were horrible, and I was not making her happy. I never cheated on my wife during our marriage. In retrospect, I often look back at all the mistakes that I made in my life.

My biggest regret was that I didn't spend more time with my two girls and gain their love and respect. My wife told me I would die a lonely old man, and she was probably right.

Being a street cop for such a long time changed the way I think. I will now try to explain my daily thoughts, which are because of my ever-present hypervigilant state of mind. I still have a strong mistrust and suspicion of most people I see in public. I often think of worst-case scenarios, such as an active shooter or some other type of emergency while I am in a crowd of people.

I still try to think of what actions I would take in various situations. I haven't carried an off-duty gun for over thirty years, so running is always at the top of my list.

Mike and his two young daughters, Amber on Right and Serena on Left.

## Chapter 58
## The Bomb Squad

When I joined the K-9 unit, I also was selected to be on the bomb squad at the same time. I soon found myself at Redstone Army Depot, in Huntsville, Alabama, where the FBI's Hazardous Device School was located. It was the only facility in the nation that trained police officers about bombs and explosives.

The first day the instructors told the class they were serious about sending students home that failed the written or practical tests. The school was no picnic. In every class, several students were washed out and sent home for various reasons. I was determined to not be sent home. That would be embarrassing.

Cops from all over the country attended the month-long school. It was interesting to hear that there was little difference in police work when talking with cops from LAPD to NYPD over a beer or two. Most departments of any size throughout the country have the same problems.

I studied several hours every day in the bar with the other students and made several close friends. Saving money by eating the free snacks during happy hour and trying to act cool in front of the ladies, when I knew I wasn't, was my nightly ritual while at bomb school.

Two NYPD cops were the funniest guys you could ever meet. The stories these guys told over a few beers would keep you laughing all night long. They were very young and married, but had no problems picking up the ladies. These guys got more action in one month than I did my entire life, which wasn't much.

They also aced every test they took and never seemed to study. Years later, I found out they had the luxury of being able to study ahead of time. They had copies of all the tests. A student from an earlier class wrote down every question and answer after he took his tests during the instructor review. They got his test copies, with the answers, and studied them prior to taking their own exams.

The FBI got wise to the high scores some agencies always seemed to get each class. Things soon changed. Each new class got a set of test questions that were different from the previous classes.

Cops are like anyone else in society. Some will cheat to get what they want in life and others won't. At some time, an officer's immoral acts, in one form or another, has caused a problem in every agency in the country.

Fortunately, police background investigators discover and eliminate most undesirable police officers during the hiring procedure. Unfortunately, it is impossible to find all dishonest police candidates who should never wear a badge.

## Chapter 59
## The NYPD Story

One night at the bar, two NYPD cops who were also attending the bomb school told me the funniest cop story I had ever heard. They pleaded with me to not repeat the story because some of the cops involved were still working as managers and chiefs of NYPD.

I always did have a big mouth and could never keep a secret and wasn't home more than a month before telling other officers the funny story. I didn't know if the story was really true and would never see the two NYPD guys again, anyway.

They told me that four guys from their department were driving an unmarked vehicle back from a police conference they attended in a southern state. The four in the car were a captain, who was driving, a lieutenant, and two sergeants.

They had just eaten dinner at a pizza parlor and had more than one pitcher of beer. The captain was driving around eighty MPH because they all were tired and wanted to get home. They still had a couple hundred miles to drive and wanted to make good time.

He looked in his rear view mirror and couldn't believe it when he saw those fucking red and blue lights. They were being pulled over for speeding by a state trooper.

The captain was a quick thinker and tossed his handcuffs to one of the sergeants in the back seat. He told him to put the cuffs on and take his lead as he watched the trooper walking up to their car.

This was not some local cop pulling them over. It was a state trooper. He was 6'6 and weighed about 250. His shoes were shined, and his uniform was impeccable. The trooper explained that they were stopped for speeding and requested the driver's license and registration.

The captain showed the trooper his badge and told him they were transporting a cop killer, sitting in the back seat, to Attica state prison. He said they were speeding because they wanted to get the piece of shit out of their car as fast as they could.

The trooper was very professional and told the captain he was sorry for the delay, and they could be on their way. He then asked the captain if the officer the guy killed had any kids. Wanting to make the story sound good, the captain said, "Yes, he had two kids and his wife was pregnant."

The state trooper shook his head and started walking back to his unit. As he walked by the car's open rear window, he reached in and punched the handcuffed sergeant in the mouth. He said, "Have a nice day asshole," and walked back to his squad car and drove away.

The sergeant was so pissed off they didn't take the cuffs off right away. He kept saying he was going to kick all their fucking asses for laughing so hard.

## Chapter 60
## Close Call for Texas

Most of our class met every night in the bar for the free food and the local girls, who were mostly bomb technician groupies. The groupies all seemed to have kids who needed a permanent daddy. Most of them didn't want a date; they wanted to get married. They knew our class schedule before we arrived in town.

We heard stories of some past students at the Hazardous Device School. Some had fallen in love with one of these groupies. They quit their jobs, divorced their wives, and moved back to Huntsville, Alabama, to live. That's the truth. I was told by the instructors that this happened more than once.

For most guys, a month is a long time to be away from your wife and sex. A lot of the non-cheating types in our class weakened towards the end of the month. We would see them dancing with one of the regular girls, who we all knew by first name. After a few drinks, we'd see them leaving together hand in hand.

This one older cop from Texas was a very straight arrow. He didn't drink much and never used bad language. John was a nice guy and often talked about how much he missed his wife and two young boys. John was religious, and made it a point to go to church on Sundays, even while at school.

On Friday night of our third week, we saw John dancing with one of the few good-looking ladies, who rarely came into the hotel lounge. This was the first time anyone saw John even talk to a girl, let alone dance with one.

I was jealous because all I ever danced with were the old ones who looked like my mother when the lights came on. Sheep didn't come into the bar, so I didn't have much luck that month.

The next day was a Saturday, our day to study around the pool for our next test. John showed up late, and we were all curious how his night went after he left the lounge.

John looked embarrassed and didn't want to talk about it. That was his mistake, being around five drunken cops and not wanting to talk about some good-looking lady he made it with. It took some pleading from the horny cops that just wanted to know what happened.

He said he was scared as hell when he invited her to his room for a drink. When they got to his hotel room, they had several drinks, and he was shaking like a leaf. He explained to her he had always been faithful to his wife and wanted to remain so.

She said she understood, and they had an innocent kiss. The kiss started getting more heated than a little peck, so they stopped. John now was hornier than a two-peckered Billy goat.

John again explained that he wanted to remain faithful to his wife. He then asked the gorgeous lady if he could just see her breasts. John wanted to be platonic and didn't want to touch them. The lady, who was a nurse, removed her shirt and bra, revealing the most beautiful tits he had ever seen.

The guys then asked him what happened. John was not smiling and looked down as if he were going to cry. He looked up with a little grin and said he really did not plan on doing anything with her. John then said he wound up fucking her all night long.

She had just left his room before he came out to the pool. I then noticed a young lady with two small boys standing behind him. He turned around and was stunned to see his family, who flew out to surprise him. John later told his classmates that his wife didn't find out about his fling. Talk about a close call.

Days later, he told us something that always stuck with me. John said it was the best sex he had in his life, but it was a mistake. He said he felt so ashamed and dirty he couldn't look his wife in the eyes. It wasn't worth it.

## Chapter 61
## I Hate Spiders

I graduated from Redstone and now was a bomb technician. Just like in police work, I was a rookie all over again. The FBI's basic bomb school was just the beginning of years of studying and reading. I went to many specialized schools all over the country and learned a lot of different things that had to do with explosives and bombs.

I went to a conference of selected bomb technicians to discuss electronic countermeasures, which is a secret way of jamming the frequency of a remotely operated explosive device.

The British bomb experts in this specialized field were flown in from England to discuss tactical considerations. I was surprised to learn how important secrecy was to the British Officers, who took their profession very seriously.

In the United Kingdom, their military handles all the bomb calls. The hard lessons learned by the deaths of many British bomb technicians have saved countless lives in the United States. The English bomb technicians are some of the most highly trained professionals in the world.

My favorite class was at the explosive entry school in Arizona. I learned how to use the minimal amount of explosives to breach a door or wall. We were taught that speed, surprise, and violence of action were our goal.

More departments nationwide are using tactical breaching, once the stigma of using explosives is mitigated. Explosive breaching is a lot safer than using a sledgehammer to open a door. Using a robot to blow out the door lock was a common tactic we used.

One cold, windy, winter night, I heard the phone ring at four in the morning. I knew it was a bomb call-out and answered the phone. The dispatcher told me that a body had been found under a freeway underpass.

The homicide detectives wanted the bomb squad to respond because of a possible explosive device found near the body. I responded to the scene with Sam, an old-time bomb technician.

We were still half asleep when we pulled up. The area was blocked off with yellow crime scene tape. Sam and I were briefed by the lead detective.

The detective said the body was a young male in his twenties that appeared to have been in the bushes for several weeks. A brief case next to the man had four galvanized metal pipes inside that looked like pipe bombs.

Sam and I walked up to the dead guy. Thank goodness it was winter because he could have smelled a lot worse. The victim's shirt was blown off, leaving his bare chest exposed.

He had three perfectly round holes in the middle of his chest. The holes were the same size as the pipes in the briefcase. Sam and I examined the briefcase and found that one pipe still had a live 12-gauge shotgun shell inside, which we removed.

A suicide note next to the victim said he did it because he was dying from aids. The man constructed the device using four pipes, each containing a 12-gauge shotgun shell.

He secured the pipes in the briefcase with glue and wire. The shotgun shells were designed to go off at the same time once a fishing line was pulled. The fishing line was connected to four sets of springs, which held back homemade firing pins.

His plan almost worked perfectly. He held the briefcase against his chest and pulled the fishing line. Three out of the four shotgun shells fired, killing him.

One shell did not fire and had to be removed by experts. The detectives had no idea what kind of device they were dealing with, which was why the bomb squad was called out to the scene.

Sam and I had just removed the live shell and were looking down at the poor bastard, when we saw something that was straight out of a Stephen King movie. The homicide detectives were still standing out of the danger area, while Sam and I looked down at the pale white skinny body. A large daddy-long-leg spider crawled up from the bushes onto the man's torso.

Both of us said nothing as we stared at this creepy creature. The spider then crept up the man's chest. As if in slow motion, the spider stepped into one hole, one leg at a time, until he disappeared in the man's body. Sam and I were a little shaken by this gruesome spectacle.

We still said nothing as we continued to stare down, wondering where the hell the spider went to. Both of us stared in disbelief when we saw the spider creep out from a different hole than he went into.

The spider then crawled down the man's chest and back into the bushes. I had heard of midnight snacks before, but this was ridiculous.

## Chapter 62
## The Big Bomb

Several years later, I got one of the strangest callouts a bomb technician could ever experience. It was seven in the morning on a Sunday when I got the call. The dispatcher only told me that a bomb was found inside a closed muffler shop in a bad part of our city.

The owner of the shop told the police he went to his business early Sunday morning and found an atomic bomb inside, and had no idea how it got there. Raising just a little suspicion, the patrol cops called the bomb squad.

I was the senior bomb technician and my brand new sergeant was fresh out of Redstone. The new sergeant arrived several minutes before I did. Once I arrived, my young sergeant stopped me outside the business.

The sergeant told me to look inside the bay of the muffler shop because we may have a problem. I looked around the work area and didn't see any obvious device, just a large oval-shaped metal container on a trailer.

I told the sergeant that I couldn't find the device. The sergeant knew about the military and some of the weapons and bombs used.

His father was a lifetime serviceman in the Airforce.

The sergeant told me, "Hey dummy, go look at the thing on the trailer." He was serious, and had already told the patrol guys to evacuate the immediate area.

I climbed on the trailer and started looking at this huge metal tank. The end of the tank had funny looking fins attached, and it looked like a big military bomb of some sort.

I wondered what kind of bomb was this big, and how did it get inside a closed muffler shop on the weekend without the owner's knowledge? I asked the sergeant if there was any possibility it was live, and what kind of bomb he thought it was.

The sergeant said, "It's a Fat Boy atomic bomb." The sergeant told me to write all the numbers on the side of the bomb and call the FBI. Being the bomb squad senior technician, I asked the sergeant if we could just counter charge (blow up) the device in place.

I said we were in a bad area, and we could drop the city's crime rate by half. We didn't know any of the million people who lived in that bad part of town, so what the hell? The sergeant didn't like my smart-ass suggestions, and told me to make the calls.

I called the FBI, who must have thought it was a joke. The agent told me they don't handle atomic bombs, and I should call the Air

Force. Then he hung up on me. I then called the closest Air Force base. Trying to talk to someone about a lost atomic bomb on a Sunday morning was quite the challenge.

After being transferred to several people on the phone, I finally got the full story from a military EOD supervisor. The bomb that we had inside a muffler shop was, in fact, the third atomic bomb that was built to be dropped on Japan if they didn't surrender during World War II. A part of history, many to this day, still don't know.

I was told the bomb was from their base and was inert or not active. It was being transported to a military museum in the southern part of our state. The Air Force had subcontracted a private party to transport the bomb from their Air Force base to the museum several hundred miles away.

We later found out the entire story. The truck driver had some minor engine trouble while traveling through our city. He knew of a good friend's muffler shop nearby because he had worked there before. He also still had a spare key to the business.

The driver was going to park the atomic bomb inside the muffler shop for an hour or so while he got the part for his truck's engine. He didn't think there was a need to tell his friend that he was going to park a bomb in his shop, because it was Sunday and the business would be closed. The driver never expected his friend to go to his shop on a Sunday morning. He did!

Law enforcement bomb squads have always been trained to call a Military Explosive Ordnance Unit to handle any and all military ordnances, foreign or domestic. Highly trained bomb technicians from various military branches have the needed expertise to handle these things. Civilian bomb squads are trained to evacuate, freeze the scene, and call for a Military E.O.D. Unit.

Mike wearing his Explosive Ordnance Disposal Unit pin. The bomb squad pin was the same at the military's EOD pin. Mike received bomb training from the military EOD specialist on numerous occasions while attending schools at military bases throughout the country.

Atomic Bomb named "Fat Boy" found on a trailer inside a muffler shop in North Sacramento on March 13, 1990.

## Chapter 63
## September 11th, 2001

I can still remember the sunrise of September 11th, 2001. Bruce, a friend of mine in the bomb squad, called me early in the morning while I was sleeping.

By the way his frantic voice sounded, I knew something was wrong. He said to turn on the TV, our country was under attack. Then Bruce told me I was to come to work as fast as I could, then hung up.

My mind was still in a fog when I turned on the TV in the bedroom, waking up my wife. She sat up in bed and asked me what's going on? I told her I wasn't sure.

We both sat in silence as the national news channel was replaying a video of a passenger plane hitting one of the World Trade Center towers. The TV then switched back to a live shot of the struck tower. A very large hole could be seen in the side of the tower, with smoldering fire inside.

The first thing I heard was that it may have been an intentional act. The national TV announcer said there were several other passenger planes on the east coast that were also off course.

It wasn't more than a few minutes after I woke up and was watching live TV with my wife, when the second plane hit Tower Two of the World Trade Center. It was so unexpected my wife let out a high-pitched scream of surprise and said, "My God, no." I never felt like that before in my life.

My stomach felt like it jumped out of my body because I knew I'd just witnessed numerous people on the plane being killed. God only knew how many people died inside the building on the plane's impact.

I had no idea what was going on. My wife, who was born and raised in New York City, was now crying and our children were already in our room wondering what was going on. She knew I had to go to work like so many times before, but that was just part of being on the bomb squad.

Once I got to work, I was assigned to use my dog for various explosive detection searches throughout the city. As I entered our office, the other bomb squad guys were watching live TV and listening to the various reports of several other missing planes with possible terrorists aboard.

Again, for the second time in a few hours, my stomach turned upside down when I watched the first World Trade Center's unexpected collapse to the ground. We were all taken by surprise, as we never thought the structure was in danger of a complete total failure.

It was sickening to think about how many lives of innocent people were lost while I watched the building fall straight down. I knew hundreds of first responders like the medics, police officers, and firemen had to have been killed when the tower came down on them.

That tragic day only seemed to get worse, as we saw the second tower collapse a short time later. We didn't say much to each other at first because I think we all were a little shocked.

That day changed the bomb squad community more than anything in the history of our nation. Soon all bomb technicians had to attend a variety of schools presented by the federal government. Chemical, biological, and radiological classes were all part of the mandatory training.

Bomb technicians had to go back to Redstone every other year for mandatory recertification. In addition, after 9/11, bomb technicians regularly received assorted training throughout the country.

Large vehicle bomb, suicide bomber, and chemical weapons schools were all basic training for bomb technicians after 9/11. The federal government also provided each bomb squad in the country with numerous expensive items, such as robots, x-ray machines, and explosive detection equipment.

I was very proud to be a bomb technician in Sacramento. Our bomb squad was the first Metropolitan Bomb Squad in the country. It was established in the early 1970s and consisted of bomb squads from the local federal, state, and county law enforcement agencies. Each of the bomb squads trained together twice a month, and shared equipment and personnel when necessary.

I really enjoyed being on the bomb squad for twenty years. I had many good times attending schools and training with the area bomb technicians. Playing with high explosives and blowing things up twice a month was a dream job that any guy would love to do for a living, I think?

Over the years, many advancements in equipment and technology have taken place in the bomb squad community, making the job much safer. Robots are now routinely used in many situations which prevent anyone from risking their lives.

Prior to the availability of robots to do most of the dangerous work, a bomb technicians had to rely on a hundred-pound bomb suit to keep them safe.

Bomb technicians were trained to wear a bomb suit when walking up to a suspicious package or possible explosive device. They would then have a little protection when they X-rayed the package or device. Now robots do these things remotely.

## Chapter 64
## Unabomber

One afternoon, I was giving my two girls a ride home from school in my bomb vehicle, because I was on call. I was listening to the police radio when a call about an explosion with a possible fatality was dispatched. The call location was at the California State Forestry building, in the downtown area.

I dropped my two girls off at home and rushed to the scene of the explosion. Our new bomb squad sergeant was already on the scene, with an old FBI bomb technician, who I knew well.

The FBI agent told me he thought the explosion may be the work of the Unabomber, because of the type of state business that was bombed. The Unabomber was the nation's most wanted man at the time.

He had sent or placed many bombs throughout the country, killing and injuring several people over many years. The agent then made a cursory walk through the blast area. He soon discovered pieces of burnt strapping tape around the seat of the explosion. This type of strong tape was one of the signatures the bomber used.

His devices were usually designed to explode when the victim opened a package. He used the strongest tape available to secure the package tightly closed, so it didn't go off when he was carrying it around.

The FBI agent was one of the more down-to-earth guys I had ever known. He was an old timer that worked under J. Edgar Hoover at one time. A lot of new young FBI agents have very little police experience when they're hired.

On different occasions, young agents have pissed off some of our older cops. The rookie agents acted like they were deities because they wore FBI raid jackets.

Fortunately, experience is golden. We had one of the FBI's oldest bomb technicians with us. We all got along very well, and the post blast investigation only took several days to complete. FBI took all the evidence, which was all right with us since it was their case.

The old agent told us that all the FBI's national post blast response teams were in Oklahoma City. The Federal Building in Oklahoma had just been hit with a several hundred-pound car bomb, killing a lot of civilians.

He asked my sergeant if our local bomb technicians could help the FBI process the scene. They were lacking all their experienced explosive investigators, who were at Oklahoma City bombing. The scene was sealed off, with the victim still inside.

It was obvious the victim died quickly because of the major blast injuries he sustained from the explosion. We all knew it was important to take things slow. The first thing we needed to do was to make a plan on how the post blast investigation should be conducted.

The FBI would be the lead agency, with the local bomb technicians helping to collect and preserve the evidence. I knew my bomb squad sergeant was fresh out of Redstone and had little post blast experience. He was a former Marine and a lot older than I was.

The sergeant was the bomb squad's liaison with our department's managers and the various other bigwigs from the state and local departments that responded. He let me and the other bomb technicians do the grunt work, while he kept everyone else out of our way.

One postal inspector showed up, wearing a pair of white cotton gloves. He told the old FBI agent that it was his crime scene, because the device was sent in the mail. The Inspector then started to walk into the building without asking anyone.

He was told to stop by my sergeant because it was FBI's crime scene. The postal inspector became upset and argued that it was his crime scene. He again tried to walk inside the building, at which time my sergeant stopped him for a second and last time.

My sergeant told the inspector that it was the FBI's crime scene, and if he attempted to walk inside the building again, he would be arrested. The inspector must saw the serious look on the sergeant's face and knew he wasn't kidding around. The inspector then left the scene, still wearing his white cotton gloves.

A plan was developed and the two-day processing of the scene began. The other bomb techs and I were assigned to process and collect evidence from the blast seat. It was summer and the body still was in place.

It didn't bother me at the time to pick up small pieces of the victim's body. I was on auto pilot for forty-eight hours, thinking only of my investigative responsibilities.

I helped the deputy coroner pick the victim's body up. We placed him on some sheets and then into a body bag. This was not a normal duty for me.

Small pieces of flesh from the victim were falling out of his torso when we put him on the stretcher. I picked the body parts up and put them inside the sheets, trying to act professional.

The smell was overpowering. I almost threw up inside the body bag, which would have compromised any evidence found inside with the victim.

Several days later, I thought about what I saw. I almost threw up and thought about the victim's family. I later learned the victim who was killed was a devoted family man. It always bothered me when innocent people died.

His wife and two sons loved him very much. He was a little league coach and the nicest person you would ever want to meet. There was no reason this nice, innocent father and husband should have died at the hands of a mad man.

I learned from the witness statements about how close several other people in the office came to dying that day. The package came in the mail.

A pregnant worker who picked up the package felt something was wrong with the way it looked. Several people stood around the package while she handled it.

She told a male employee about the suspicious package and was told to put it down. The package was addressed to the prior president of the forestry service, who no longer worked there. The head supervisor, who was in the lobby area, was told about the package. He told the other employees that he would look at it.

He attempted to open the package, at which time it exploded, killing him. It was fortunate that he was alone when he tried to open it. Anyone else in the lobby would have also been killed.

The bomber constructed his device from a metal pipe, which he serrated. The serrations caused to it fly apart into many deadly pieces when it exploded. The inside walls of the lobby were peppered with holes from the flying pieces of the metal pipe.

Later, the suspect was arrested in a small cabin in Montana. He eventually confessed and pled guilty. He received life in prison, a light sentence for our nation's most notorious serial bomber.

The lead federal prosecutor later gave the local bomb technicians an eight-hour class on the unknown facts of the serial bomber. I don't even want to mention the suspect's name, other than asshole.

The suspect was an evil genius. He kept a diary of all his bombings and also wrote a lengthy, rambling manifesto of his thoughts about life. His manifesto was his downfall, as he demanded it be published in a national newspaper.

The suspect's brother recognized several phrases in the manifesto that only his brother used. One phrase he used, in a different way than other people, was the main give away. He used to say, "You can have your cake and eat it too." This was backwards from the way the phrase is usually used.

His brother used to send his hermit brother small amounts of money because he felt sorry for him. He lived in a tiny cabin, grew his own food, and kept to himself. Once the brother realized he may have been giving support to the nation's most wanted man, he called the authorities to report his suspicion.

I can't begin to imagine how hard it was for him to turn in his own brother, regardless of his crimes. He knew his brother would likely face a death sentence.

It is easy to hate someone who does something bad when you don't know them. Not loving a family member even when they have done something wrong is a hard thing to do.

It didn't take long to track the suspect down and arrest him without incident in his cabin. A forest ranger who the suspect knew, often walked by the cabin. The ranger knocked on his door one day, and when the suspect answered, he was arrested without incident by the FBI's SWAT team, which had been hiding outside.

The suspect knew about DNA. He didn't lick the stamps he used on the packages that contained his deadly devices, which were mailed around the country. He even found a single hair on the floor of a bus depot. Later he placed it on his next bomb, as a false DNA clue. The suspect glued shoe soles that were larger than his size, to the bottom of his shoes, in case he left a shoe print impression.

A diary was written in a secret code, which at first could not be broken by the FBI. They sent the coded diary to the nation's best code breakers, who also could not decipher it.

The experts said it was one of the most sophisticated codes they had ever seen, even during World War II. Luckily, the key to his code was found in his cabin, so all of his notes could be read.

He wrote in his diary, "My devices were becoming more powerful." The suspect conducted his experiments in the woods by his cabin. He was a self-taught bomber, using scraps of wood and pipes as his container. His bombs were cheap but deadly. Most of his bombs were victim activated. When his packages were opened, they blew up.

He experimented with a mixture of potassium chlorate and aluminum powder, which turned out to be an extremely powerful explosive. The devices were becoming more deadly with each new incident.

The suspect gave a lot of thought and planning to each of his bombings. He didn't care about the three people he killed or the dozens of others he scarred for life. One thing is for certain, he was not going to stop his senseless bombing of innocent people. He had absolutely no concern who opened one of his bombs.

After the deadly bombing we had a plague of suspicious package calls throughout the city. Many times, the reporting person said they felt embarrassed calling the police about something that turned out to be nothing.

I would always tell people the same story I was taught at Redstone. The instructor said a bomber from the IRA (Irish Republican Army), who planted numerous devices during his reign of terror, once said: a bomb technician must be lucky every time they deal with an explosive device. The bomber has to get lucky only once.

People were told to never open any package that they think is suspicious in anyway because there is no margin for error when it comes to a bomb. Any cop would be happy to smile at the unexpected gift that a person receives, rather than responding to the call of an explosion and finding a mangled dead body.

Buddy on Mike's lap in the Bomb Squad Office. He's growling at a vacuum cleaner.

## Chapter 65
## FBI's Top Ten Critical Incidents

The FBI compiles statistical information from law enforcement agencies throughout the country for a yearly report on the top critical incidents:

• The violent death of a partner in-the-line-of-duty
• The dismissal or loss of the job
• Taking of a life in-the-line-of-duty
• Shooting someone in-the-line-of-duty
• Suicide of an officer who is a close friend
• The violent death of another officer in-the-line-of-duty
• A murder committed by a law enforcement officer
• A duty related injury such as a shooting
• A violent job-related injury to another officer
• A suspension from the job

During my career, I was involved in eight out of the ten listed incidents. Maybe that's why I went a little crazy? I also survived several very close calls with death when different suspects tried to shoot, stab, and even throw me off a ten-story building.

I was seriously injured six times over the years, requiring code three ambulance rides to the hospital emergency ward. On more than one occasion, I was nearly killed while being the lead police vehicle during one of my many late-night K-9 pursuits.

Hazards come in many different ways in law enforcement. As I've said before, in the beginning of my career, a young officer, who I knew, tried to grab his service revolver after it fell from the inside of his locker just before swing shift roll call. The gun accidentally discharged, killing the officer instantly.

Not many officers went through as intensive a career as I did, but a lot of cops I knew developed the same problems I had. Slowly departments realized the need for training officers how to handle the stress of the job. Officers now routinely have classes on their mental health and how to cope with the pressure of being a cop.

Police officers are a microcosm of the public. They worry about paying their bills on time and have family problems just like everyone else. The biggest obstacle to mental health in our society is the stigma of fear that follows a person when they ask for help. This is no different for a cop or any other person. No one wants other people to think they are crazy.

The Blue stigma of seeking help in law enforcement is fading away, but has a long way to go to help the many cops who have sustained serious injuries to their minds, such as PTSD.

Mike and his 3rd dog, Buddy during his last year in the K-9 unit.

## Chapter 66
## Meeting Moses

One of the things I often did on the bomb squad was to use my K-9 to conduct explosive searches or "sweeps" for visiting politicians, dignitaries, or any other VIP that came to town.

The bomb sweeps were usually conducted at least an hour before the VIP's arrival. After the sweep, a patrol officer would be posted at the location to ensure the area's safety.

Normally the rooms to be searched by my K-9 would be checked to make sure they were empty prior to the inspection. On this occasion, I was searching the VIP suites at the Arco Arena prior to the governor's inauguration ball.

As I entered one small suite with my dog, I saw an elderly man dressed in a tuxedo sitting on a couch reading a book. The man had his shoes off, and his legs were stretched out on a small table in front of him.

I told the obvious VIP that I was there to conduct a fast bomb sweep of the room. The very nice man said he understood, and watched me as I walked my dog around the room for a short time. After I finished, the man asked if it was okay to pet my K-9, as he loved dogs.

At first, I wasn't sure who the old guy was while he petted my dog. Then I suddenly recognized his voice. There was no mistake about who he was when I looked at him a little closer. It was Moses himself, or better known as Charlton Heston.

I must have had a surprised look on my face because Mr. Heston just smiled at me for a few seconds. He then thanked me for my service and shook my hand before I left the room.

In my career, several presidents, movie stars, and famous sports figures walked by my post when they were in town. They were busy and never talked to me or the other officers providing security.

On one occasion, I had a conversation with a Secret Service agent about Bill Clinton. The president was in town giving a speech when I talked with the agent in the Down Room. This is a break room provided to law enforcement personnel.

He was assigned to protect President Clinton, and I knew he wouldn't say anything bad about him or he might be reassigned to the North Pole. I asked him what kind of guy was the president? The agent told me the president was a very nice man in person. I asked him what he liked to do for fun.

He said the president loved to play golf, and he often played with John Daley. It's funny, both men had questionable situations occur during their careers. Maybe birds of a feather do fly together, or at least play golf together.

When I was at an explosive entry school, called Gunsight, we were told Tom Selleck was at the same school for a week. It was a large facility located in the desert and he was in a different area learning how to shoot.

At the end of a long hot day blowing doors open, we were having a few beers during a barbecue at the range. A truck pulled up and a big guy wearing an old grey cowboy hat stepped out and asked for a beer. There was no mistaking who it was.

Tom Selleck stayed for dinner and talked with us for over an hour. He was as down to earth as you could get. We asked him if he would take a picture with us, which he gladly did. I still have the framed class picture on my desk, which includes Magnum P.I.

## Chapter 67
## Goodbye Old Friend

Not long before I was due to leave the force, I got a phone call from an old, retired friend who was now working for the district attorney's office as an investigator.

Nick was one of the few friends that would call me up to chat and fill me in on anything new going on in the department. As an investigator, he heard what was happening in the department more than I did.

He told me he had some bad news. Gale had terminal cancer, with only weeks to live. I had known many friends that died, but this hit me a little harder. Gale was only fifty-eight years old and was always so full of life and energy. It was hard to believe he was dying.

Gale was the older cop that wrote me a letter of commendation for a pursuit I helped him in during my first year in the department. It was the first pursuit I called out on the radio. This is when Gale kicked the guy in the nuts because he had a gun.

Nick told me that Gale was at home and liked having visitors. I searched for hours for the commendation letter that Gale had written

for me over thirty years ago. I found the type-
written letter that had turned yellow over years.

It was a full-page letter containing all the
details of the pursuit and arrest. It was not very
common for one officer to take the time to write
a nice letter for a rookie officer.

Over my career, I would write numerous
letters of commendation for officers that did a
good job during an arrest. I was just trying to
pay it forward as a result of Gale writing a letter
to me as a rookie.

I went and saw Gale the next day. Another
retired cop from my police academy was
visiting when I arrived. Gale was heavily
medicated, but still able to hold a conversation.
It was obvious his mind was foggy, and he
didn't have long to live. His family had a
hospital bed set up in the living room, so he
could look outside.

Gale didn't seem to remember me, as it
had been five years since we last saw each
other. He was still glad to see any old cops
from his department. Then I showed him the
letter he'd written so long ago.

His eyes were also going bad, and he
couldn't read it. I read the letter out loud to
Gale, who sat up in bed and began to perk up
a lot. He remembered the pursuit very well and
told me details of the arrest that I had even
forgotten.

Gale had a big smile when he explained how hard he kicked the suspect in the nuts when he wouldn't get down. He told me he often thought of that pursuit over the years as one of the best arrests of his career.

I left him saying I would visit the next week. We both knew we wouldn't see each other again. Gale died soon afterwards at home with his family by his side.

During the many funerals for my retired friends, I think about the times we had on the department together. My pals and I went on a lot of crazy calls the public wouldn't believe actually happened.

It's nice to have memories of being parked next to a good partner while taking a fast cat nap in some dead-end street. Between radio calls we often talked about the close calls we had with suspects during an arrest and how much force we used on the guy.

An emotional bond develops between people when they go through life and death situations together. After a shooting, most cops would rather talk to another cop who has been in prior a shooting themselves, than a trained mental health professional. This is because they know the other cop can Identify with what they're going through, because they have experienced the same thing.

## Chapter 68
## The Wagon

When I had less than two years to retirement, a good friend asked me to partner up with him, working on the drunk wagon. I had known Mitch for twenty-eight years. We played on the same softball team and partied together on many occasions. Both of us just wanted to coast our last few years. We would just drive around and pick up drunks, and then take them to the detoxification center or jail.

This was the easiest job in the department. We were number one and two in seniority of all the department's patrol divisions. On the second day working with Mitch, something very strange occurred.

I had a dream that night that something life altering would happen to both of us while we worked on the wagon together. I told Mitch it would not be a shootout or anything violent. It would be a lifesaving thing, or something that had to do with a death. We never talked about my dream again, but it wasn't long before it came true.

Most people think of street derelicts as bad people who don't want to help themselves. Nothing could be farther from the truth. Mitch and I met some of the nicest people you would ever want to meet. It's true they were all sick with alcoholism, but they weren't all bad people.

We found ourselves giving out small amounts of money and cigarettes to our favorite drunks, who needed a helping hand. On more than one occasion, we gave a beer or two to the ones who had the shakes to keep them from having a serious medical issue of alcohol withdrawal.

We made some very close friends with some of the street drunks we picked up out of the gutter each week. They would always thank us for taking them to detox instead of jail. At detox, they had to stay for several days and dry out and sober up, which a lot of them wanted. The jail would only hold a drunk for four hours and then out the door they would go to get another drink.

We liked this old fart that always talked about the ladies he had sex with during his life. One day, we were transporting him and a female drunk to detox. We knew the lady well. She had a reputation of giving a blow job to anything with a penis.

Once we arrived at detox and opened the rear door to the wagon, we saw that her reputation was justified. She was giving a blow job to the smiling old man like there was no tomorrow. We shut the door and let them finish in peace and hoped like hell no one found out about it. The old fart couldn't thank us enough once we opened the door. We now had a friend for life.

One old drunk named Jerry was a Viet Nam war hero. He was a crew chief in a helicopter and saw more than his share of death. Jerry talked about some of his experiences, but usually started crying over his friends that were killed in the war.

One day, we found out Jerry had a bad stroke during the night at detox and was taken to the hospital. Mitch and I visited Jerry several times during the next few weeks because we knew he had no other friends or family in town.

Jerry was soon placed in a long-term care home because he couldn't walk. Mitch and I visited him one day and gave him a framed picture of us standing next to the wagon.

He couldn't talk very well because of the stroke, but he didn't have to. The tears in his eyes spoke for themselves and we understood how much the picture meant to him. Jerry died several weeks later.

Mitch and I stopped becoming so attached to the street drunks because it was too painful to lose a good friend. People just see and think of the bad side of the drunk lying in the gutter.

What they don't understand is that each person has their own story to tell. Jerry never once bragged about the lives he saved in the war, but it was clear he never forgot the ones that died.

Mitch and I had more fun with the drunks every day than we could believe. These guys did some of the funniest things imaginable, which kept us laughing all shift. We started liking the drunks more than some of our arrogant cops.

It pissed us off when we saw some rookie officer treating a street drunk like a piece of dirt. More than once, we told off a young officer about being disrespectful to our clients and friends. The young cops would look at us like we were crazy because they just didn't understand.

Mitch had been divorced for several years and had a twelve-year-old daughter he shared custody with. His daughter, Shelly, was the center of his life. He would call her daily from work when she wasn't staying with him.

Mitch would brag about his daughter every day. He was a very proud father. He often would call his ex-wife to make sure their daughter was going to the dentist or other important appointments. Mitch was a great dad who spent as much time with his daughter as he could when he had custody.

Mitch and I talked about taking care of our elderly moms. We both had moms with dementia, which made for interesting stories each day. We loved sports and talked about our favorite teams all the time. He invited me to a professional baseball game when the season started up.

I learned a lot about Mitch, working with him for ten hours a day, for almost two years. We talked about every subject under the sun and didn't always agree.

He was a special friend who I shared my problems with. Mitch gave me great advice about my relationship with my daughters. He also was very concerned about my health issues. Mitch was like a brother to me.

## Chapter 69
## Homeless People

Working on the drunk wagon gave me a new insight into the homeless people that I worked around every day. I learned that most homeless people share many commonalities in life.

Most street people have a combination of substance abuse problems and mental health issues. Many times distressed homeless people get involved in minor disturbances and are put on a 72 hour hold for a mental evaluation.

Police officers transport them to a secure mental health facility for treatment. After a doctor's evaluation, many mentally disturbed homeless people are dumped back on the streets because they did not meet the legal criterion to keep them against their will in a mental health hospital.

If the doctor deems them not to be a danger to others, a danger to themselves, or gravely disabled, then they are turned back out on the streets, no matter how "crazy" they actually are.

The homeless population commits numerous minor violations of the law that can severely affect property values in any city. Basic sanitation issues, such as taking a shit in front of a store, have always been a concern to business owners.

Most homeless people have criminal records, little education, and few work skills. Many of the street people have had family members who tried to help them come home, but they gave up long ago.

Some cities give the homeless free places to stay on the condition no drugs or alcohol are allowed. People who have a long-term substance abuse addiction and a mental health concern will not stay in any location that prevents them from getting high.

Simply put, no city in the nation could afford long-term placement of their homeless population, in order to help them with their substance abuse issues.

The concept of one on one, tailor-made treatment and counseling for the homeless mental health issues is unrealistic and probably impossible to implement. This is because of the noncompliance of the homeless in attending the sessions for very long.

It is very important for people seeking to stop a substance addiction of any type to have a good social support network. Family and friends may have a strong influence on many people who try to stop an addiction.

People with substance abuse addictions, coupled with diagnosed mental health issues, need specific individual treatment. The treatment must be tailormade, in order to be affective.

This type of treatment requires a long-term stay at a professional recovery center facility. One on one counseling will be needed on an ongoing, daily basis. These programs range in costs, but are usually very expensive. Because of the high costs of the needed treatment, most people with jobs can't afford the recovery centers.

Even after completing a several month term treatment program with mental health professional counselors, many patients fail to recover. The homeless population usually has little or no social network to help them recover.

Family members don't want them around and their friends have substance abuse issues of their own. The homeless receive little help for their mental health issues.

If any city could afford treatment for all the homeless, it still would fail. People who have substance abuse problems and mental health issues are not going to voluntarily stay at any treatment facility, no matter how nice it is, unless it is locked down, like a jail.

Again, no city has the resources or money to treat the homeless population's substance abuse addictions and mental health issues. It is a sad commentary that being "out of sight and out of mind" may be what the homeless population and the city government both wants. Homeless people who have lifelong mental health problems will not get cured overnight under any circumstances. The growing problem will only get worse with time. Moving the homeless from one location to another is just a quick fix to stop the justified complaints from neighbors and business owners. Finding a long-term solution to the immediate homeless problem is a complex issue which will likely not get better.

This is because of the many individual problems the homeless have. For many homeless folks, asking other people for money to get drugs or alcohol for the day is more important than their next meal or where they're going to sleep.

## Chapter 70
## The Phone Call

I had to have a surgery to control an irregular heart rhythm, which kept me off work for several weeks. Mitch called me the day after my procedure, which cheered me up, as I didn't have many friends.

The next week, I didn't have my phone with me when Mitch called and left a short voice message. The message was just asking how I was doing, and he would call back. I got sidetracked and did not call Mitch back that day.

Two days later, a lieutenant from the Internal Affairs Unit called me at home. The lieutenant, Neil, was one of my closest friends in the department. I trained Neil when I was a training officer.

Neil was a fast riser and a very bright officer. He soon promoted to sergeant, and later was my K-9 supervisor for several years. Neil was a company man and the most ethical person I had ever met. His morals could not be compromised. He treated everyone fairly, which is all anyone could ever ask.

Neil sounded funny when he talked to me on the phone. Then he came to the point and told me something which changed my life. Mitch had just committed suicide. He left his daughter a goodbye note and hung himself in his closet on the day of her eighth-grade graduation.

I had that sick, numb feeling I had experienced when my dad died. The pain was unreal as I realized I never called Mitch back after his voice message. I will always be plagued with guilt for not calling him back. I will never know if my friend was reaching out for help during his time of pain.

There was speculation about why he killed himself; however, no one knew for sure what the reason was. It really doesn't matter why he did it. At first, I was sad, and then mad at him for doing such a selfish act. How could he do that to his family and daughter?

After days of trying to come to grips with his death, I understood his pain. During my divorce, I once was so distraught after an argument, I put my gun to my head for a few seconds.

I was alone in the house and was in so much mental anguish that I didn't want to live anymore. I just wanted the pain to go away. That's when I thought of my mom.

How could I hurt her that badly? I remembered the promise to my dad to take care of her. I put the gun down and knew I needed help. I then understood, Mitch was in some horrible pain he couldn't make go away. He chose the easy way out for him, but left his daughter with a lifetime of questions that can never be answered.

I have often wondered about that dream I told Mitch about on the second day we worked together. After I spoke at his funeral, I realized what the dream was about.

My dad had an obvious premonition the night before he died in my arms. He was feeling no pain that night, and typed his last Will and Testament. He left everything he owned to Fluffy, our family cat and Jimmy, a mentally handicapped neighborhood boy. It sounds preposterous, but I think premonitions may come true at times.

## Chapter 71
## Instructing Other Cops

After Mitch killed himself, I didn't want to go back to work. I was assigned a desk job at the police academy because I was still having issues with my heart. I was also taking a blood thinner and the risk of bleeding to death if shot or injured was too great to work the streets.

While working my desk job, a female sergeant, who worked part-time as the head of the department's peer support team, contacted me. Sandy worked well helping other officers who had been traumatized by a critical incident. She asked me to be part of a newly formed peer support committee. It felt great to help other cops. I knew my bad experiences in the department could help other officers from making the same mistakes.

It was the best possible therapy for me to recover from the guilt I had over Mitch's death. I blamed myself for not calling him back after I heard his message.

For the last twenty years, I had taught bomb classes up and down the state to thousands of civilian and sworn personal. I was a good instructor, with a sense of humor that at least kept the students entertained during my classes.

I loved to teach; however, I doubt that any of my bomb classes saved lives or even helped many people all that much. Now was my chance to make a difference in helping brother and sister officers.

For the next year, I poured my heart, soul, and a lot of my own time into writing proposals for a full-time peer support unit. I looked at a dozen different agencies' orders and policies and drafted numerous suggestions for our department.

Because of my partner's suicide, I became involved in the Peer Support Unit, and started teaching SMILE (Stress Management in Law Enforcement) classes to sworn and civilian employees. The topics I picked for my class were all things that made me a crazy K-9 Cop. The fact that I lived through and experienced each of the topics in my class gave me the needed credibility with the students, by providing them with firsthand accounts of what happened to me during my career.

Many other authors have impressive platforms, titles and educational degrees following their names. The most important aspect that qualifies me to write this book is my real-life experience with each of the topics.

Some realities are best learned by listening to someone who has experienced what they are talking about. My class was about why cops kill themselves and other mental health issues. I read many studies on police officer suicides while working light duty,

I wanted the most recent and accurate information for my class. The FBI's Behavioral Science Unit had completed a comprehensive, detailed report, which was exactly what I needed.

I researched the FBI's study on officer suicides, conducted by their prominent Behavioral Science Unit. I also investigated the many other common mental health issues that affect officers each day.

The sergeant was one of my best friends and let me work on my class as much as I needed. He knew my class was important, because we had two officers commit suicide within a year of each other.

I printed one copy of the FBI study on officer suicides on the academy's copy machine. I wanted to read it and pick out interesting material for the class. I didn't look at how long the study was when I found it on the internet.

I went to lunch and came back to the academy, only to find the printer still copying my suicide study. The sergeant was standing next to a stack of papers that was twenty-four inches high. It was my study, and it still was not

done. It must be the largest study in the world
to be that big, I thought.

The first words out of the sergeant's mouth
were "What the hell are you doing?" He was a
little more than pissed off that I was using most
of the paper supply for the academy.

The sergeant was known to be a penny-
pincher. He was a great guy and saved the
department money when he could. The amount
of money wasted by officers on the little things
is amazing.

I explained that I didn't realize the study
was that lengthy, and I would be more careful.
He really wasn't upset because he knew I was
hurting inside and took pity on me. The study
filled four large binders.

In the class, I talked about my divorce and
alcoholism. I told the stories of my suicidal
thoughts, and about the one night I put a gun
to my head. I was candid about the many
mistakes I made in my career. I told them
about neglecting my family because I was
always thinking about the job. A lot of the
students identified with my messed-up life and
appreciated my honesty.

After class, students would often approach
me on the side to share a bad call they had.
Some of the students had never sought
counseling and had never spoken to anyone
about the bad experience they were involved

in. This was the first time they let it all out, and some even cried.

I continued teaching for several years after I retired. I taught officers about the psychological dangers and hazards that are all too common in every police department in the country.

My extreme passion to help other people and pay it forward in life set me apart from most instructors. I obtained my in-depth knowledge of psychology through years of extensive investigation and research.

To have a crying person hug and thank you is an unforgettable experience. It was healing for my own soul. I knew I had hurt so many people in my life, and it was now time for me to pay it forward. I soon was a happier person.

Helping another person in life is just an extension of helping yourself. The intuitive feeling of connecting with another on a personal level is what inspired the instructor to design and teach this course.

A wise man once said,

"You may never remember who you laugh with"

"But you will always remember who you cry with."

I found this to be true.

## Chapter 72
## Suicidal Thoughts

The last year of my marriage was a living hell.
The loud arguments about little things were
becoming more frequent, usually ending with
one of us leaving the house for a few hours.

I hated to argue with my wife and drinking
seemed to help, or that's what I wanted to
believe. After one awful fight, I found myself
drinking more than I usually did.

My wife left the house with the girls,
leaving me alone to cry up a storm and feel
sorry for myself. I was positive my wife was
having an affair, which she was, but I still loved
her even though I was deeply hurt.

I was in our bedroom, sick at the thought of
my wife having sex with another man. Sitting
on the side of the bed, I opened up the small
headboard cabinet and removed my off-duty
handgun.

I put the barrel to my right temple, thinking
one fast squeeze and all my pain and sorrow
would be over in a flash. Then I got scared and
thought, what the hell was I was doing? I
thought how bad my mom would feel if I killed
myself and put the gun away.

In an effort to show why some cops kill themselves, I have included a small portion of the FBI's study. Unfortunately, the skills to survive the emotional aspects of a police career are given far less attention relative to officer safety training.

### Suicide Statistics

- Every 54 hours an officer is killed in the line of duty.
- Every 22 hours an officer commits suicide.
- Officers going through a divorce are five times more likely kill to themselves.
- Handguns are used 80% of the time, due to 24-hour accessibility.
- The dangers of the job rank very low as a cause for officer suicides.
- Personal relationship problems rank as the number one reason.
- 70% of cops who commit suicide have alcohol in their system.
- Suicides at home are the most common location.

### Major Factors
- Relationship problems
- Job difficulty (discipline/ suspension)
- Alcohol/substance abuse

- Psychological problems
- Financial problems

## Chapter 73
## Staubing Your Dog

Recently I had lunch with several friends who were about to retire after putting in thirty years in the department. It was fun to talk the about old times and the crazy calls we handled together.

John was one officer I knew well because we worked the same shift together for many years. He asked me if I remembered a K-9 class I taught at his academy. Then John reminded me of a funny story I had long forgotten.

I taught numerous bomb and K-9 classes to thousands of cops from various departments over a twenty year period and forgot many stories people reminded me of.

This story was different because it had been retold around the department for several years. In fact, it became a K-9 unit legend that was both true and humorous.

John remembered me bringing my dog, Bear, to a patrol K-9 class I was teaching at the police academy. The class was filled with thirty-five brand-new officers who looked like they were just out of high school.

Back then, young officers in the academy stood at attention when any instructor or member of the academy staff entered the room. They always said *sir* when asking questions, and were serious about learning what was being taught.

There was no playing around at the Academy. They all knew they could be washed out for the smallest thing, like being rude to an instructor.

John said a student by the name of Staub asked me a question. Before he continued, I assured him I remembered the story very well.

It started when Staub politely raised his hand during my class, then asked the most embarrassing question I've ever heard in my entire career.

Staub asked me if I ever masturbated my dog to raise his sperm count. He said he'd heard that was done to help impregnate another dog. My dog was lying next to the wood podium located at the front of the classroom while I gave my lecture. I looked down at him and saw that he was watching me for the first time during the class.

The other students in the class let out a collective moan when Staub was done with his question. Some of the students were snickering and smiling, while others were looking straight down.

I had never heard that question before and didn't know if was true. I didn't know how to respond because I was a more than a little surprised. After a moment of silence, I looked at my dog and said, "You would like that, wouldn't you, boy?"

Trying to act as professional as I could, I explained that I didn't know that much about K-9 sperm counts. The class was now falling out of their chairs from laughing so hard.

I continued with my regular lecture for a few minutes until the class started laughing again while staring at my dog. I looked down at my partner and saw he was licking his fully erect penis. He did that from time to time just because he could, I suppose.

Talk about being embarrassed. I know my face was just as red as his dick. I yelled at him to stop that, but he was in another world of his own. There he was, blissfully going down on himself, while I stood in front of the class waiting for him to finish.

The class was now in stitches from laughing so hard. I asked one of the students to let me know when Bear lit up a cigarette, so I'd know he was done.

Several days later, another K-9 handler said my K-9 class story was going around the department. He said people were asking him if he'd ever "Staubed" his dog before.

People asked me the same question for years. I always explained that I never "Staubed" any dog in my life, but I'm sure some of them didn't believe me.

## Chapter 74
## The Right Path

A few months before my planned retirement, I had some chest pains after teaching a class one day. Another instructor in the room took one look at me and knew something was wrong. I was put in a car and taken to the emergency ward.

I was rushed into the hospital on a gurney and hooked to an EKG machine. They instantly saw my problem. My pulse rate was way too fast, and my heartbeat was irregular. The doctor said I was in atrial fibrillation. He also said I needed a cardioversion immediately to prevent me from having a stroke.

By now, I was very scared. I thought I might be having a major heart problem, which I was. The doctor said I needed a shot in my abdomen to thin my blood. Then he would use a defibrillator to shock my heart back into a normal sinus rhythm.

The next thing I knew, I woke to a beeping sound and found myself connected to a multitude of wires on my chest. The sign on the grease board said I was in room 205 of the cardiac intensive care.

I spent a week in the hospital and was given a series of heart tests by several cardiac specialists. The city doctor who reviewed all my heart tests and lab results explained that the stress of the job for the last thirty years had severely weakened my heart.

He said if I didn't retire soon and get immediate control of my blood pressure, it would surely kill me. The news hit me in the face like a ton of bricks. I didn't want to retire, but sure didn't want to die either.

The doctor explained that the prolonged stress I experienced during my career took its toll on my heart and I needed to rest. I never wanted to stop being a cop because I still loved my job very much, but knew it was time to retire.

For some cops, playing golf every day after their retirement is their idea of happiness. After I retired, I tried to play golf as much as possible for the first six months. Unfortunately for me, I am a perfectionist. I learned golf is a very humbling game. I had to practice almost every day in order to get better, but barely noticed a difference in my score card.

I had many good times playing golf after my retirement, but something was lacking in my life. For some strange reason, I felt something was wrong since I wasn't doing anything meaningful. I had an overwhelming need to have some type of value or purpose in life.

Most retired cops have family responsibilities to keep them busy. Others have a strong social network of friends, or a hobby that takes up most of their time. I have lived a very reclusive life, with just a few close friends.

My mom always called me four times a day after my dad died. She was always very lonely with few friends to talk to. Her dementia got progressively worse over the years, causing me concern about her living alone.

While on duty, I tried to stop by each night to check in on her between my radio calls. At least once a week, I would have my Code-7 at her apartment and watch TV with her. We always watched Jeopardy and Wheel of Fortune because those were her favorite game shows. She wanted to be on one of them someday.

One winter night, I called her to warn her of the freezing weather the next morning. I told her the sidewalks may be slick with ice, and to be extra careful on her morning walk. I don't know if she was paying attention to me or not, but the next morning, she fell on some ice and fractured her arm in several places.

Due to her osteoporosis, or thinning of the bones, the doctor advised me that another fall would likely lead to her death. My grandmother died in a convalescent hospital, and I knew, if at all possible, my mom would never go to one. I remembered the promise to my dad, to take care of my mom, a promise I planned to fulfill at all costs.

I, like the other retired police officers, have often encountered several forks on the road in life. One path was the right path to take, and one path was the wrong one. I always knew which the right path was, but I never took it.

The reason I never took the right path was because "it was too damn hard to take." It was easy to take the wrong path. It took me a long time to learn that walking on the right path in life is simply helping other people, but some things are easier said than done.

I soon came to another fork in my life. I chose to take care of my mother after she fell. I no longer had a life of my own, as any fulltime caregiver will tell you. You always eat last.

People said I was a good son for taking care of my mom. I disagree. I think it's a duty of any son or daughter to take care of their elderly parents, if at all possible. It's simple; just the normal circle of life. Our parents took care of us when we were young, so we should take care of them as they get old.

I decided to take care of her after her fall. Learning how to cook, wash clothes and do many other household duties was the easy part of caregiving. But I didn't find that out until later.

Hypervigilance, P.T.S.D and an ugly divorce after a twenty-nine-year marriage all contributed to mental insanity. However, nothing could have prepared me for being a fulltime caregiver for my mom, who was rapidly, physically, and mentally, declining from Alzheimer's.

Her stay in the hospital seemed to affect her mentally. She came home confused and had problems with her short-term memory. My mom had moderate cognitive impairment, MCI.

She could remember details of events that took place in her childhood extremely well. My mom was so proud of me being a police officer. She used to tell everyone she met about her son.

My poor mom wanted to live by herself and start driving again. She desperately wanted her independence and hated being a burden on anyone. My mom couldn't walk unassisted because of her poor balance, which made her a bad fall candidate. She had to be held by the arm to steady her when she walked.

My mom's greatest fault was her stubbornness. She insisted on not using a walker of any kind. I bought her the Cadillac of walkers, but she never used it much.

Her dementia got worse. No one can understand the pressure and how hard it is to live with someone you love that has dementia. It is like going through Chinese water torture, when one drop of water would fall on the victim's forehead until they went crazy.

I would get one drop of stress at a time, twenty-four hours a day, seven days a week. It was the little things that drove me stark raving mad. She would often ask me for a piece of candy, ten times in a five-minute period.

Explaining she was twenty-five pounds overweight, and didn't need to eat so much candy, didn't do any good. After hearing her start crying, I would give in to her requests and give her all the candy she wanted.

Dressing her every day, only to find her trying on something else once I walked out of the room, was always a challenge for me. She wanted to wear a long sweater on a hot summer day or no coat when it was freezing out. Arguing about what she should wear was something that I didn't look forward to every morning.

One day, she again asked for several pieces of her favorite candy after eating a large lunch. I gave her two chocolate candy kisses, which she ate immediately. Within seconds, she asked for two more candy kisses. I told once again she should not have any more candy because of her weight gain. My mom cried and said I didn't love her. This was all it took to drive me over the edge.

I reached up with both my hands and pulled two very large clumps of hair out of my scalp. Looking down at the gobs of hair in my hands, I thought, my God what did you just do? I had gone truly crazy.

It was hard for me because I knew she didn't understand that the stress of taking care of her was literally killing me. I was giving her the last few years of my life, with complete dedication to taking care of her every need, and she didn't even know it.

Having tremendous guilt for yelling at her when she was driving me over the edge of sanity was all too common. The daily, hourly stress would be so bad sometimes, I felt like I was going to pop inside. I started to have suicidal thoughts again, but couldn't ignore the promise to my dad to take care of my mom.

I researched contacts for various social services for caregivers and the elderly. It wasn't a lack of money which stopped me from hiring someone to help. My mom was a very proud lady who had her dignity. She still wanted to live by herself and drive a car. I couldn't stand to think of a stranger taking care of her. That would have destroyed her will to live.

I couldn't let my mom's happiness be compromised by letting someone else do the work that I could do myself. I pray I did a good job taking care of her until the end of her life. She was truly the kindest person I ever knew, and I was extremely lucky to have her as a mom.

It comforts me to know that I did my best and kept the promise to my dad. We all will meet soon again, in some way or another. Death is just a process, a beginning of something we don't understand.

## Chapter 75
## Racism in Police Work

Most unjustified police shootings or use of force complaints are because of poor training, and a fear of being killed or hurt. Racism accounts for some wrong doings in police work because it is impossible to weed out all racist cops.

Being publicly scrutinized by the media and the lack of support from city hall causes resentment in many officers. Another problem may arise when cops become afraid to pull their guns when they actually should. A tragic outcome will soon occur as a result of police officers nationwide being unfairly fired or even prosecuted for making an honest mistake during violent confrontations. There will be a few officers who unfortunately hesitate to shoot or use deadly force when the situation appropriately calls for it, ultimately costing those officers their lives.

In most questionable cases of accidental deaths or unintended injury by the police, research has revealed these tragic events were caused by critical errors in judgement made during violent encounters. Studies have shown poor training greatly contributed to unfortunate deaths and injuries, including of minorities.

Changes in police work are often caused first by poor tactics used by officers, followed by an extreme public outcry for justice. It's a sad fact that cops will always make honest mistakes that unfortunately end in tragedy.

Police work has changed significantly over the last fifty years. From the heavy-handed, semi-military tactics used in the 1960s, to the present day community oriented policing concept, cops, now more than ever, see the vital importance of building relationships with all members of the public.

Today's police officers are learning about cultural differences and increasing their understanding of specific problems in minority communities. Throughout our nation, police departments have been focusing their efforts on building good community relationships in all minority neighborhoods.

Today, police officers are more professional than they have ever been. They receive specialized training in using nonlethal options, which makes the public much safer compared to years past. Officers also regularly receive in-depth training on verbal de-escalation techniques.

Cops receive implied bias training, which explores the hidden prejudices that all people have. Cultural awareness and public relations are common areas of importance that officers are taught to be sensitive to.

Law enforcement has slowly evolved into an honorable line of work because of comprehensive hiring practices designed to recognize and weed out racially biased candidates. No other profession in the country goes through the extreme lengths that law enforcement agencies do to prevent racist people from getting hired.

It may be hard to believe, but racism in law enforcement is one of the lowest of all professions. No police chief anywhere wants a racist cop to be hired, because their unacceptable public behavior will eventually reflect back on them, ultimately costing the chiefs their jobs.

All police departments go to extreme efforts to not hire anyone who shows any racial biases for several reasons. When a bad cop gets hired, they can spoil a department's reputation in one incident. Departments train background investigators to be vigilant for any negative racial biases that would lead to a disqualification.

The hiring process has several stages designed to identify and disqualify any racist police candidates, including a one-year probationary period where the applicant can be fired without cause. Any signs of racism detected during the extensive hiring process would be an automatic cause of dismissal.

The first thing in the hiring process of all applicants is a comprehensive background investigation. Highly trained background investigators thoroughly examine school records and employment history, then conduct personal interviews with each prospective police candidate.

One of the background investigator's primary jobs is looking for any reports or signs of racial biases or tendencies. If the police candidate passes their background investigation, they will then take an extensive written psychological test.

Those who satisfactorily score on the written test will proceed to a personal interview with a trained mental health professional. The written test and oral interview are designed to recognize subconscious biases, which may lead to disqualification.

The police candidate will have to pass an oral board as well as a physical agility test and complete a full medical examination. After passing all the tests and interviews, the police candidates still must score high enough among the other hundreds of other qualified candidates to get the job.

During the probationary period, police trainees will be assigned to several Field Training Officers for six months. Each F.T.O. will evaluate and report their police trainee's progress by completing daily and weekly written performance reports. Any signs of racial abuse or excessive use of force during the officer's probationary period would be an automatic cause of termination.

It would be hard to find any other job or profession in the country that takes the extreme measures to find and disqualify people with racist biases or tendencies that most law enforcement agencies do.

I never wanted to work around racist cops because their bigoted words and actions made my job much more dangerous. The vast majority of the honest, hardworking police officers would all agree it only takes one racist cop to destroy years of devoted work by the whole department.

Racism brings anger and dislike directed at the police by all the minority communities, which jeopardizes an officer's safety on every call. When a police officer treats anyone unfairly because of their skin color, it paints a bad picture of every cop who wears a badge, as well as the entire profession.

During my career, I heard the "N" word from more than one officer. I am ashamed to publicly admit that I am one of those officers. My impulsive nature got the better of me more than once. I used that awful word just to fit in and impress some of the bigoted white cops I worked around.

Each time I used the vile expression, I felt like a small child who said a dirty word. I knew it was wrong to use that term, but I wanted to be accepted by the older cops. Looking back at my career, my immature attitude to impress others was something I will always feel guilty about because my dad would have been ashamed of me.

When I was growing up in the 1960s, my father's best friend was an African American. On many occasions, he came to our house with his family for a barbeque and to play cards. I never saw any difference when playing with his kids or any of my other friends of color.

One night when I was young, the national news came on as my family sat in front of our black-and-white TV. I witnessed police abuse for the first time in my life. I didn't understand why the police treated black people so violently during a peaceful demonstration.

I can remember seeing two police dogs biting one old man at the same time. The man was screaming in pain and was not resisting arrest. Even as a small child, I knew this was wrong. I later learned what the protest was about.

On May 2, 1963, young black civil right protesters walked out of the 16<sup>th</sup> Street Baptist Church in Birmingham, Alabama, and started to march to City Hall. At the end of the day, nine-hundred-fifty-nine people were arrested.

Their ages ranged from six to eighteen years old, because adults could not afford to take the time off work to protest. The next day, even more students joined the peaceful march. At that time, the Commissioner of Public Safety for Birmingham, "Bull" Connor, gave the okay to use fire hoses and police dogs on the protesters.

This extreme, unwarranted use of force was captured on TV for one of the first times, and shocked millions of Americans. People of all races immediately called for the fair treatment by the police during peaceful demonstrations and marches.

TV revealed police abuses, such as the unnecessary use of force and acts of violence to control crowds of people during peaceful demonstrations. It quickly changed the way people received their news. Watching Walter Cronkite soon became a nightly ritual for my family and millions of other Americans throughout our country. Americans were stunned by the tactics used by the police on peaceful protesters.

Watching the violent police tactics during peaceful protests, marches, and demonstrations changed the way people looked at law enforcement in general. Unfair treatment by the police would no longer be tolerated.

Fortunately, this type of misconduct slowly started changing, mainly because TV reported and exposed the wrong doings of the police during the evening news. These visual images changed the way society viewed the police and a new generation of liberalism was born.

Police pursuits, violent confrontations, and officer involved shootings are now frequently seen by millions of Americans on the nightly news. Capturing never before seen police activity on TV has shocked the public at how aggressively the police respond when their life is threatened.

Now different cameras capture an officer's every movement once they step out of the station's door. Most patrol vehicles have dashboard cameras, and patrol officers all wear body cameras, which record every contact they make.

From the moment an officer steps out the station door, they all know their every word and action is being recorded on either their patrol car's dashboard camera or their body-worn camera.

Police officers are all very conscious that every public contact they make during their shift, including traffic stops and all radios call for service, will be permanently recorded and stored for any potential accusations of police misconduct.

Cops today understand any use of force, such as a shooting, will be criticized and condemned by the public before the investigation has even started. Before potential witnesses have been contacted and evidence is collected, the public will cry for immediate answers and want officers fired or arrested.

Officers know any use of force they use will be highly scrutinized and reviewed by their supervisors and their individual agency. They also know they could lose their jobs, face legal charges, and go to jail if they violate a person's civil rights or break any law or the violation of department policies.

Cops today don't want to take the chance of doing good old-fashioned, proactive police work for fear of making an honest mistake and then being fired, sued, or even arrested. Officers all know they will be caught on some camera if they do the slightest thing wrong.

Contrary to popular belief, many cops suffer depression and have a hard time after seriously hurting someone or taking a human life. It's even more difficult for cops to deal with psychologically when they are publicly accused of a racially motivated death or serious injury by their own mayor or city council members before the case has been investigated.

It wasn't that long ago, after the horrible 9-11 terrorist attacks, that police officers throughout our country were treated as heroes. But how fast we forget about their everyday bravery and dedication to a dangerous and thankless job. It's painful for police officers to be looked at as the enemy by young and old people alike of all races and cultures now.

Many police chiefs throughout our nation are very aware there is no widespread systemic problem with racially motivated white police officers. Unfortunately, many honest, hardworking police chiefs are afraid to admit this fact because of their fear of being viewed as unsympathetic to minority communities

## Chapter 76
## Today's Police Officers

Without a doubt, I could not have been a police officer in today's world. I was lucky I didn't have to take a polygraph test back in 1978 when I became a cop. My heavy pot smoking would have been a disqualifier. Truth be known, I have often wondered if I should have ever been hired.

I was very lucky there were no cameras used in law enforcement when I was a cop. During my career, I may have used more force than I should have during a few arrests. There is no statute of limitations for civil rights violations, which makes my memory vague.

Many times, I was alone during a violent struggle with a strong suspect who just got of prison. I didn't bring any cover officers with me during my K-9 searches because they often interfered with my dog. I had to stay focused on finding the suspect and not worry about an officer getting bitten.

When I used too much force, it was out of fear of being killed or seriously hurt. As a common practice, I wanted to use speed, surprise, and violence of my actions to take suspects into custody. Being a nice guy could get you killed in police work.

Thanks to television and the ubiquitous presence of cameras, police work has evolved and changed into one of the most extremely honorable profession anyone can have, contrary to whatever the public may think.

Reading an exciting police novel or seeing a popular cop movie doesn't tell the true story of what it's like wearing a badge. In the movies and on TV, cops routinely get into shootouts, when in reality most cops never discharge their weapon during their entire career.

What the public doesn't know is that a street cop's day is filled with countless boring hours of report writing and booking evidence, only to be interrupted by the occasional moments of fear, excitement, and addictive adrenalin rushes.

People have strong opinions towards law enforcement that are based on their personal experiences. From receiving a traffic ticket to reporting a home burglary, most public contacts with the police are surrounded by a negative circumstance.

The public now expects cops to perform their duties like robots. They should not make mistakes during life and death encounters and shouldn't show any emotions while being spit on by the public they are paid to protect.

Cops today are not allowed to show any emotion or anger during a physical assault or confrontation. Cops all know if they make an honest mistake, they may be unfairly criticized by the public before the appropriate investigation has even started. Lack of public support and harsh criticism by the media has fueled a dislike towards the police in general.

Cops now realize they must report any type of abuse they see other cops commit on or off duty, or they risk losing their jobs, being sued, or even going to jail. Officers also know they may have to step in while on a call and take immediate action to prevent acts of misconduct by other officers.

Officers today don't want to take the chance of making self-initiated arrests for fear of losing their jobs or going to jail. Patrol officers now just handle the radio calls for service in their district and write a few traffic citations.

Police officers hesitate to follow up on their valuable gut instincts when observing someone suspicious. These are just a few reactions caused by the lack of public and departmental support felt by many police officers nationwide.

Today's police officers are trained in the many areas related to the nationally accepted Community Oriented Policing philosophy. This includes learning about different cultures as well as better understanding minority communities. Officers also regularly receive in-depth implicit bias training, inclusion training, as well as learning non-violent verbal de-escalation techniques.

A famous psychologist (Abraham Maslow) once said, "96% of what we do in our conscious life is greatly affected by our subconscious thoughts and desires." In my class, I taught students how to recognize their own subconscious or implied biases that all people have. Students gained a new perspective on why they treated certain people the way they did.

Learning simple psychology in order for officers to better understand their own subconscious biases is a good thing. Recognizing and understanding their own differences is paramount for effective communication.

In order to survive a long career in law enforcement, police officers need to become emotionally resilient to the psychological toll the job takes. The cumulative effect of going to numerous suicides, homicides, and horrible car crashes can have an overwhelming and lasting negative consequence on a cop's life.

The potential psychological damage done to many officers after they see hideous things during a critical incident, or a bad call is something every law enforcement agency needs to address. All officers should learn how to use simple psychology to better help other cops and the public, after they have experienced such an incident.

When a cop shows an act of compassion during a time of crisis, a person's positive outlook on the police will change for life. Helping people in this manner is much more significant in building a meaningful relationship with the community than the best arrest an officer can ever make.

Technology is changing core aspects of how we interact as a society, and as society changes, so too will the tools, techniques, and concepts the men and women of law enforcement use to keep us safe.

Innovation is not just about the latest gadget—it's about finding new ways to do things better. Innovations can take the form of new concepts, new methods, or new tools.

The innovations that are shaping the future of law enforcement begin with emerging technologies that support new concepts of operations, enabling the interventions, and relationships that keep our society safe.

## Chapter 77
## Influencers

Many special people helped me throughout my life. They influenced the way I thought and changed me, both before and after I became a cop.

Both my parents were special in their own ways. Mom liked all people, no manner what color they were or what lifestyle they led. She had the biggest heart and always shared with others throughout her life, from handouts to homeless strangers to volunteering her time for many different charities. I tried to be like her because she was so well liked by everyone.

She taught me to be a nice person. One of the important lessons I learned from her was to give all people I talked to a compliment and try to make people feel special about themselves. Treat everyone with high respect and try to make each person smile.

My mother said it was important to learn to be a good listener. Give people your undivided attention and don't ignore what they say. She said to always respect other people's viewpoints, even if I disagreed with them. I should treat people the way I wanted to be treated. My mom told me helping one person never changed the world, but helping one person can change their world. No one ever became poor by giving.

My mom also gave me one of the most important lessons in my life—learning true humility. She taught me humility does not mean I will have a low opinion of myself. It meant to accept myself for my good qualities, as well as seeing my limitations.

She said it was essential for me to understand that I was no more or less important than anyone else. She said every human is equal and I should show humility to other people. I should never put myself above others in life.

I may be biased, but my dad was the most intellectual person I ever met. He had a way of telling stories that captivated people. During his short life, he changed the lives of people around him. I will always remember our deep talks about the existence of a higher power.

He loved animals and nature and going camping. My dad was more like my best friend growing up than my father.

My dad taught me to get in touch with nature each day. Take the time to smell a flower or watch a bird or animal. He said I must learn to feel my common connection with all people and every living thing.

I was taught that people need to peacefully co-exist with each other and learn to live in harmony with all the living world. Staying balanced in nature is mandatory for the survival of mankind.

My father explained our human minds are cluttered with daily concerns, which prohibit us from coming in contact with nature or our common energy source.

He told me that when I see a bird in a tree or watch a beautiful sunrise, I can feel a connection with nature, because in those fleeting moments of spiritual self-awareness, I am one with the universe and am in the presence of God.

\* \* \*

Aunt Barbara is my mom's youngest sister. She is one of the pleasantest people on earth and doesn't have a mean bone in her body. Barbara was an elementary school teacher for over forty-one years and helped thousands of young kids to read and write. But most of all, she taught her students how to give each other respect. She was the epitome of a true role model for anyone to follow.

My aunt taught me lessons that were not found in any schoolbook. She told me I was not born with a purpose. I must first find my purpose by discovering and recognizing my own abilities and talents. She said she had found her purpose in teaching kids each day for so many years.

Barbara told me I would not discover my purpose in life by doing the same things over again. She was exactly right. As a recovering perfectionist, I define my purpose in life as a continual journey of becoming the best possible version of myself. By doing this, I can help other people become the best possible version of themselves.

My aunt told me that being happy and living the best quality of life is a purpose I may choose. Providing for my family the best I can is an important purpose to have in life. Barbara taught me that happiness is something that's unique for every single person, just as our purpose in life differs from all others.

\* \* \*

I was a shy kid with no confidence about anything I did during my freshman year in high school. Mr. Ruben, my philosophy teacher, taught his students about great thinkers such as Socrates, Plato, and Descartes.

I was mature for my age and liked this special old man. We shared many talks throughout my high school years, which gave me the confidence to believe in myself. He told me I must try new things in order to find my potential in life, my hidden abilities, and natural talents. The trick was in finding out what naturally attracted me.

Mr. Ruben taught me to be the first one who steps up to the plate and thinks out of the box in order to get things accomplished on the job. This helped me later with my working relationships with all my supervisors.

Gaining self-confidence improved my public speaking skills by teaching me not to hold my tongue when I had something important to say. A very small percentage of people find true purpose in their jobs. Finding something positive I liked to do each day was critical for my happiness and overall well-being.

\* \* \*

Sam Chan was my uncle. He grew up in a small village in Canton, China where he learned how to fish and live a simple life with his family.

Sam came to San Francisco as a teenager and met my Aunt Lola. He married her during a time when interracial relationships were frowned on by people of all colors. Sam was like my second father. He and my dad had a special relationship, as if they were blood brothers.

We used to visit the Chan family or they would come to see us at least once a month for most of my life. I was close to my two cousins and my aunt, but there was something special about Sam. He taught me many things in life that helped me along my way.

Sam said the most important thing is knowing what was most valuable in life, and prioritizing accordingly because living the best quality of life should be my main mission.

He once asked me what I needed in life. "Food, a place to live, and clothing to keep warm are all basic necessities," I said. He said that providing for my family's needs by keeping them safe, comfortable, and free from hunger, should also be one of my goals.

He told me not to spend too much time at work because my family and I would face the unintended negative consequences. I didn't learn that lesson very well and worked a lot of overtime in order to buy my family extra things. I wish I'd realized that they needed my time and company much more than any present or toy.

Sam believed that improving my physical health by consistently exercising each day, eating the appropriate diet, and getting the proper sleep should be a top priority. My good health should outweigh all other priorities in life.

He also believed that if you want to be rich, be generous. If you want to make friends, be friendly. If you want to be heard, listen. If you want to be understood by others, take the time to truly understand them. And if you want an interesting life, be interested in all that happens around you.

Sam said most people spend too much time on urgent things and not enough time on important things. He told me to do what's important first and urgent second.

My uncle learned things during his childhood that gave him the humility few people have. At the end of his life, he said in his soft voice that his only goal was to be a good person. He attained his goal and much more. His love for his family and compassion for others were passed on to them for generations to come.

Sam once saved the life of a drowning man in the river. He changed that man's life as well as countless other people. His daily actions and simple words of wisdom inspired people to be the best they could be. Sam was a very special person in my life. He gave me the insight to understand people who grow up on the other side of the world.

In many ways, my feelings for white people and our western world's lifestyle and the way we treat others pales in comparison to the respect and admiration I feel for Asian cultures and their eastern belief systems. Asian family members respect each other and take care of their elderly parents. This is not a common thing in America.

\* \* \*

Bob was a friend of my dad's who he met in college. I only talked with him a few times when I was around sixteen years old. Our talks changed the way I thought about death. He was by far the most spiritual person I have ever talked to in my life.

Bob didn't believe in any one religion or any one God. He believed in a life after death, but not like many other people do. Bob read every book written by a famous old author named Edgar Casey.

Reincarnation was something he spoke about and which made sense to me because of his simple explanation about the cycle of life. During those few talks I had with Bob, I seemed to grow intellectually. I didn't look at death as the end of my life, but just the beginning of another one.

Bob was a strange man in many ways. He had a lifetime skin disease which made his skin horrible to look at. His entire body was covered with sores, which prevented him from dating or ever having a girlfriend.

He cared for his aging mother in a large, old, two-story house on the edge of town. My dad was Bob's only friend after his mom died. He never went out, except to shop for food. My dad felt sorry for him and took him to a show on several occasions.

One of Bob's strange quirks was that he loved his five adult cats. He wouldn't even go to the show with my dad and mom if I didn't stay at his house to watch them.

I got scared before they left for the show one time. He pointed to a rocking chair in the corner of the living room and asked me not to sit in it. Bob said his mom still used the chair.

After they left, I was scared to death for the next several hours until they got back. I didn't believe in ghosts, but Bob actually thought his mom sat in the chair each day.

I learned a lot from Bob during our talks, but I told my dad I didn't want to watch his house anymore. My dad laughed his ass off, but understood my fear. It also spooked him out when Bob talked about his mom sitting in the chair.

Bob may have been different, but he was the most interesting person I have ever had the pleasure of talking to. Even at a young age, I learned some very important things from this small, fragile man.

He told me having a balanced life would give me different rewards and benefits. Staying balanced takes determination and daily practice. Too much of anything is usually not a good thing. Bob said that anything I do habitually that causes problems in my life should be considered an addiction or bad habit that requires my immediate attention.

Bob warned me that devoting too much time to any profession I later decide on would not be a healthy thing for my family. He said recognizing the critical balance between the time you spend at work and home is vital to your children's well-being, as well as your family's happiness.

He said by making daily positive affirmations and avoiding negative thoughts, it's possible over time to reprogram or rewire your brain in order to think differently and be a happier person. Bob stressed not to be a workaholic. Have positive traits, such as being ambitious and tenacious.

Having a balanced diet is just one example of how I should lead my life, he said. Understanding my emotional needs would be important for me to live a long and healthy life. He told me some needs of mine would be met through friends, while other needs would be filled by personal experiences. Bob died a young man, but his soul transcended to a higher plane of existence.

\* \* \*

When I finished the interview with the deputy chief, I left his office knowing I didn't get the job of police officer. I was very depressed because I needed it in order to get married. I walked to a sleazy bar in downtown Sacramento to get drunk. After my third beer, I struck up a conversation with a man sitting next to me. He looked like a street drunk with dirty, worn-out clothes.

Once he started talking, it was obvious this man was extremely well-educated. He had a command of the English language, which put me to shame. Prior to becoming a drunken derelict, he had been an English professor at U.C. Berkeley. He quit his prestigious job after a bad divorce and sank into a bottle.

Patrick told me his life story that day. He even told me he tried to kill himself after his divorce and had to stay in a mental hospital for several months. For the next four hours, I bought the old guy eight beers and two shots of whisky.

It was the best investment in my life. He was not only a smart man, but he had a tender heart. Patrick gave me a lot of good advice that day. He said having good mental health is just as important to my overall well-being as my physical health.

Patrick told me that learning to use the diverse areas of my brain, which are responsible for intellectual thinking, problem solving, and emotions is just as important as exercising different parts of my body, such as my arms and legs.

Patrick said for a happy life, I must have both a healthy mind and body. Most people understand the importance of daily physical exercise, having a good diet, and getting a sufficient amount of sleep. Unfortunately, most people have no concept of how important mental health is. Patrick said mental wellness has been overlooked as a critical component needed to help our children.

The negative stigma associated with seeking help from a mental health professional is a pervasive social problem that contributes to countless preventable deaths from suicides. People don't hesitate to go to the emergency ward when they become sick or injured to get a blood test or X-ray, in order to determine what is wrong with them. Unfortunately, we as a culture have failed to understand the critical importance of seeking mental health assistance when needed. This is largely due to people's common fear of being perceived as weak or crazy by other people.

I left that bar very intoxicated, but profoundly enlightened by what I just learned. I don't think I have ever talked to a wiser person in my life. That old drunk talked like a prophet. He told me things that all people should learn.

His words inspired me to stop worrying about my future because my big heart and giving nature would guide me through life. In four hours, Patrick came to know me better than most people did in my entire life. I also learned not to judge a book by its cover.

\* \* \*

Neil is still one of my closest friends. I first met him as a field training officer when he was a rookie cop. It didn't take long to see this guy was very sharp and was likely to rise in the ranks.

I thought this guy could be the Chief of Police one day. I was almost right, as he retired as a captain.

Neil later became my sergeant in the K-9 unit for several years and was by far the best supervisor I ever worked for.

I received luxuries other K-9 officer didn't get because I did what he told me to do. I didn't complain when getting bad assignments or working late hours. The other cops in our unit often whined to Neil about the smallest things, which pissed him off.

I was the one of the toughest cops in the K-9 unit and the only one who didn't question Neil's motives for his decisions or make excuses for my mistakes. I wasn't a kiss-ass, and my hard work was obvious to the other K-9 cops because I made more arrests than most of them.

Neil taught me to budget my time each day. Learning how not to rush around in life would dramatically reduce my stress and anxiety, he said. Managing my time allowed me to control my life, rather than follow the flow of others.

Good time management allowed me to accomplish much more in life and improved my productivity even when pressures were high.

Time management was the key to success. Neil said to "stay in the moment" of each day.

Staying in the present and appreciating each minute of every day, as a unique once in a lifetime experience, produced a new outlook on life for me. Living in the past brought depression, worrying about the future made me anxious, while staying in the present brings me peace.

\* \* \*

It was only by chance I met one of the most influential people if my life—a black man just out of prison. Jessie may have been an uneducated man, but he was one of the smartest people I have ever known.

Jessie never had a chance in life to succeed. The deck was always stacked against him. He never met his dad, and his mom was a prostitute and a crackhead. She tried to sell him one time to get high. Jessie had to learn how to live on the streets in order to survive.

Given a chance, Jessie could have been anything he wanted to be. He had no education, but learned more important things about life in prison than most cops or lawyers do in college. His mind could think of things which seemed to be out of the *Bible*. I have tried to pass on some of the things he taught me.

In prison, Jessie learned to meditate and stay focused on one thing, and told me to learn how to do it. He said it's a fun thing to do and would have many benefits. Meditating took me on unbelievable journeys in my mind. Learning how to stay focused in everything I did in life brought me many rewards to my professional, social, and private life. It took practice to master the art of meditation, but nothing of value comes without hard work.

By learning how to meditate, you learn how to focus your mind. It is a skill that takes daily practice to master. There are different ways to meditate and various types of meditation. Short, consistent daily meditation is more effective than meditating every other day for longer durations.

Research has shown that daily meditation invokes a relax response in our brain that has many benefits to our nervous system, such as decreasing the bad things that cause heart attacks and strokes.

Meditation also benefits our mental health by changing or rewiring our brain. Learning how to think positively decreases the neurological connections of the prefrontal cortex which are responsible for negative feelings, such as fear, stress, and anxiety. Positive thinking also helps build new connections in the brain responsible for problem solving.

The ultimate benefit of meditation is the liberation of the mind from attachment to things it cannot control, such as external circumstances or strong internal emotions. The liberated or enlightened practitioner no longer needlessly follows desires or living experiences, but instead maintains a calm mind and a sense of inner harmony.

## Chapter 78
## The Essence of Life

As a cop, I saw many things that made me question if there was a God. I learned life is not fair, and bad things happen to good people every day for no good reasons. I became bitter at the higher power that I could not understand.

Some people gain comfort and say God works in mystical ways. Letting a small child die in the family pool always made me wonder why a God would let this happen.

I have the humility to know I don't know. I believe in things I don't understand. The notion of a life after death is a popular belief that I think is true. I don't believe in a heaven or hell and a one God system.

In the previous chapter, I wrote about the wise words of wisdom given to me by people throughout my life. The things I learned from them helped me through my life. I owe it to those special few to pay it forward. I hope the lessons I learned may benefit others in some small way.

My dad taught me that the most basic instinct is survival. There is a universal law in nature that connects all living things together with a common energy source of life. Many call it God.

Just as time and gravity are common laws of nature that are woven together to form different dimensions that have not been discovered thus far, the source of life called God is also a fundamental law of nature, which is also misunderstood.

All life contains this form of galactic energy which has evolved through endless time to survive for all of eternity. God is the energy that gives life to everything that lives. This form of energy is part of an evolutionary process that has no absolute beginning, just as space has no boundaries.

God does not have a physical body or mass, but has a specific cause and effect on the entire universe, which is the survival of life itself. This common form of galactic energy exists on earth, as well as other planets and places in the universe.

God, up till now, has not been accepted as a fact of science and is still regarded by most people to be connected to some type of religious belief. At some point during mankind's evolution, they will learn God is the universal energy that connects all livings things together on earth and beyond. From the smallest microcosms of life to the tallest redwood tree, we are all part of the same thing.

My Uncle Sam taught me nature's perfection is in the ability to change the imperfections of life by adapting to each individual environment in order to survive. As in any evolving specie, humans must also adapt to their environment in order to live.

This simply means people need to peacefully co-exist with each other and learn to live in harmony with all of nature. This is achieved by balance. Staying balanced with nature is staying balanced with yourself, because you are part of every creature who flies, swims, crawls or walks on this planet.

Mankind as a species has yet to collectively understand they have a physical connection with nature and the energy of life. All people have a physical connection with each other, however, only a few people have understood or experienced the sensation of being connected to all of life.

Humans will at some point learn to feel the physical connection of all life and realize their bodies will die. However, the energy of life inside all living things is immortal. There have been a few humans, such as Jesus and Buddha, who learned to understand their connection with the maker of life. This connection to the common energy source contained inside us all is what Jesus and Buddha did at the highest level.

Jesus and Buddha both lived human lives until they experienced their own individual spiritual awakening by understanding the essence of life. Both men had very different views of God's actual existence. However, they both shared the same words of compassion, humility, and love.

Both men learned the same things after their separate journeys in nature. They discovered how to be in contact with the immortal energy source of life. Jesus called the source, his Father or God, and Buddha called the experience being Awakened.

They both learned to deny their human frailties, weaknesses, and desires in order to live a life guided by the spiritual energy of life contained inside all mortal bodies. They understood that love and compassion for all of life is nature's way of living in harmony together. Both were able to connect with their own source of life once they learned to give up their many human flaws, such as anger.

They both promoted a life of peace, love and compassion for all other people and all living things. Both followed their own individual paths to enlightenment and spread extraordinary words of wisdom to all who would listen.

They both reached a point in their lives of total spiritual consciousness. Their human bodies, made from flesh and bones, contained divine thoughts of the personal awareness and their connection with life.

Both men were more God than human at this point in their mortal lives. They rose to the next evolutionary level of mankind's existence by learning they were immortal.

My mom gave me compassion for others and to have true humility. She said they are both part of the collective essence of life that binds people together for the purpose of survival. People can live a pure spiritual life devoted to compassion for all things that live anywhere in the universe. All people have the potential to experience spirituality at a higher level.

Science has not evolved enough in today's world to prove God is a fact and not a myth. This will change in time. At some point, all people will evolve spiritually and learn to listen to the God inside them, just as Jesus and Buddha learned.

It's a slow evolutionary process of nature that only a few humans have reached so far in the history of mankind. Learning to coexist with all living things is a mandatory accomplishment necessary for survival.

I have two sides. A human side, which is largely guided by instinctual behavior and my mortal thoughts. I also have a spiritual side, which is the actual energy of life contained inside me.

My mind is cluttered with daily concerns, which prohibit me from coming in contact with the common source of life I have inside me. I must first learn how to hear a bird or see a running deer with more than my ears or eyes.

I can become a part of anything that lives by connecting with their energy of life. All people have the capability to be like Jesus or Buddha; however, only a few have chosen to relinquish their human lives in order to reach total spirituality.

It will take time for my brain to evolve away from my destructive, self-serving ways of thinking. Primitive human emotions such as jealousy, envy, and greed are still prevalent inside me, which shows I have a long way to go be for becoming an enlightened person.

Mr. Ruben taught me when I see a bird in a tree or watch the beauty of a sunrise, I can become one with nature and forget about my human side for a microsecond, because in these fleeting moments of spiritual self-awareness I can be in contact with God or the immortal essence of life.

I hope anyone who reads this will understand the energy of life connects all living things together. Our bodies will die. However, the energy of life inside our bodies is immortality.

## Chapter 79
## Paying it Forward, Advice for Young Cops

During your career as a cop, you will have rare opportunities to help many people in a variety of different ways. You may become a hero by running into a burning building to save a child. You may even get on TV for saving a suicidal person from jumping off a bridge. Those things are few and far between in police work.

A cop's career is filled with small things they do every day that the public never reads about in their morning paper. Cops don't receive medals for the little things they do.

A cup of coffee for a rape victim with that faraway look in their eyes is something that won't make the front page. The mother who just lost a child in a car accident will never forget the hug from a caring cop.

The public often desperately needs help from any cop with a heart. I believe it's a cop's job to help those who need a helping hand after an emotional crisis. Arresting crooks is the fun part of the job, but not the most important.

People will always remember the smallest details of a kind act after the death of a loved one. Their mind will absorb your kindness like a thirsty sponge. One true act of kindness will never be forgotten.

Please take advantage of the rare opportunities you will have in your career to make moments of grief a little easier for people with a small gesture of kindness. A simple warm touch is worth a thousand words of sympathy.

It's easy to think your main job is arresting crooks; however, you may be called to help some crazy old, retired cop after he fell down. Please don't become hard and cynical after seeing the bad things that you will undoubtedly experience.

Don't let the assholes of the world get you down in life. There will always be someone who treats you rudely on a daily basis. Let your feeling of love and compassion for these poor souls help them become better people.

I understand your frustrations in life. Money problems, unruly children, and elderly parents are just a few problems many cops encounter. Be grateful for the small things you have in life, for they will be the only things left after a tragedy, which ultimately hits us all.

Death is a part of life. All cops know bad things happen to good people, much too often. Going to the drowning death of a little girl during her birthday party tests your belief in a higher power. How could God let such horrible things happen to innocent people, especially children? I still haven't figured that one out.

Try not to think of the job while you're at home. Your family should always be your priority in life, even if it's more exciting to be at work. Resist the temptation to work overtime if you don't need the money. Your family needs you more at home than the department needs you for an extra hour or two.

I paid a high emotional price for the many mistakes in my career. My hope is that you will learn from them.

- Don't drink too much
- Always prioritize your family first and the job second
- Don't love the job too much
- Plan for the future; retirement will be there before you know it
- Take care of your parents; it's your duty and obligation in life
- The way to true happiness is to give happiness

I once read a story that summarizes my advice to young officers. A famous L.A.P.D. homicide detective was at his retirement dinner when the Chief of Police asked him a question.

This detective had solved many homicides during his thirty-five-year career. He was considered a legend in the homicide unit for his

intelligence and perseverance. He was one of
the best homicide detectives they ever had.
The chief asked the detective what was his
proudest accomplishment in the homicide unit.
The detective didn't hesitate for a second
before he answered the chief. He said without
a doubt the proudest thing he did in his career
was not to miss any of his two son's high
school basketball games.
The chief started to explain that he was
asking about the job when the detective
stopped him. The detective told the chief he
knew he wanted to hear about some high-
profile serial killer. He continued telling the
chief about how hard it was to not miss any of
his boys' games. The chief must have looked a
little upset with the boring answer.
The detective then told the chief how hard
it was to get fellow detectives to cover his on-
call during game nights. Many times, he had to
call the District Attorney's Office to get court
dates changed on game days. The detective
said it was a major accomplishment not to miss
one game in four years.
He told the chief that the best arrest he
made couldn't compare to how proud he felt
when he watched his boys play basketball. The
chief then realized why this man was such a
great detective. His priorities were his family
first and job second. He was the best homicide

detective because his home life was great, and he was a happy person.

Enjoy being a cop. It is the best job in the world. Don't do anything that could jeopardize your career. It will be over in a blink of an eye, leaving you wondering where the time went.

I envy all the young cops I see driving a black and white squad car around on patrol duty. A week doesn't go by without me having a good dream about working in the department. Be safe and have fun.

As a cop, I never learned how to slow down and smell the flowers. My fast-paced career was over in a flash, making me wonder where it all went. My priorities were all screwed up during my career. I learned that fact much too late in my life.

\* \* \*

I hope you have enjoyed this book as much as I had living it.